Joni Coniglio

INSTRUCTION EDITOR, KNITTER'S MAGAZINE

This is the fourth afghan in our popular series of afghans published in past issues of Knitter's Magazine. Spanning six years (beginning with our Spring 1996 issue), we've featured The Great American Afghan, The Great North American Afghan, The Great American Kid's Afghan and now, the Great American Aran Afghan.

This latest series was the result of a design contest open to our readers. Knitters were challenged to design a square using one color and some type of Aran patterning. In response, we received so many wonderful squares that it was extremely difficult to choose just 24, and even more difficult to choose just one grand prize winner!

The first four squares appeared in the Winter 2000 issue, followed by more squares in each of the next six issues. The designs feature a wide variety of techniques, from basic cables to more innovative (and often challenging) stitch configurations. (If you aren't familiar with cables, we describe the process on page 61.)

Tips 1 *Don't think of all of these squares as equals. Some are fairly simple (once you've learned how to use a cable needle) and others are a bit more challenging. They provide a perfect opportunity to try a new technique on a small scale.*

2 *All 24 squares are presented here—20 squares make up the afghan, and 4 are used in the pillows. For a view of our completed afghan and pillows, see pages 30–31. You don't need to make an exact copy of ours. Arrange the squares any way you like. You may choose to repeat several of your favorite squares, or compose your afghan with multiples of just one pattern.*

3 *Adjust the number of squares to suit your project; fewer squares to make a crib blanket or more to make a bedspread.*

4 *Due to the nature of the various patterns, all squares may not block to an exact 12" square. Although we first thought it would present a challenge when we were sewing the squares together, we found that the process of joining the squares helps to average out any differences in size.*

5 *We've given a general stockinette-stitch gauge for all the squares using size 4.5mm (US 7) needles. The needle size required for the individual squares will vary, depending upon the stitch patterns used. Check the materials listed for each square to determine the correct needle size to use. As always, the needle sizes listed are merely a starting point; choose the needle size that gives you the correct gauge.*

6 *Refer to the Knitter's School illustrations (on page 60) to assist you with methods that may be unfamiliar to you.*

AFGHAN FINISHED MEASUREMENTS
50" x 68" (including border)

SQUARE SIZE
12" x 12"

AFGHAN

Ann Stong K65	Jay Campbell K63	Hanna Burns K65	Janet Martin K64
Wicki Sever K62	Dana Hurt K63	Susan Rainey K67	Carol Adams K63
Julie H. Levy K61	Judy Sumner K61	Ann McCauley K64	Ada Fenick K66
Georgia Vincent K65	Patt Tanton Hewitt K64	Barbara Selesnick K62	Marian Tabler K61
Meredith Morioka K61	Dagmara Berztiss K66	Barbara McIntire K66	Kathleen T. Carty K62

PILLOWS

Betty Salpekar K63
Ginger Smith K64
Suzanne Atkinson K65
Ginette Belanger K62

The 5 easiest squares:

Ginette Belanger
Barbara Selesnick
Hanna Burns
Ann Stong
Julie H. Levy

The 5 most challenging squares:

Betty Salpekar
Kathleen T. Carty
Judy Sumner
Georgia Vincent
Janet Martin

INSTRUCTION EDITOR
Joni Coniglio
INSTRUCTION ASSISTANTS
Mary Lou Eastman
Jill Aurand
DESIGNER
Bob Natz
PHOTOGRAPHER
Alexis Xenakis
PUBLISHING SERVICES DIRECTOR
David Xenakis
PRODUCTION DIRECTOR
Denny Pearson
PRODUCTION CHIEF
Carol Skallerud
DIGITAL COLOR SPECIALIST
Jason Bittner
DIGITAL PREPRESS
Jay Reeve
Everett Baker
COPY EDITOR
Holly Brunner
ILLUSTRATIONS
Carol Skallerud

Tenth Printing, 2014
First Published in the USA in 2003 by
XRX, Inc., PO Box 965, Sioux Falls, South Dakota 57101-0965

ISBN-10: 189376217-3
ISBN 13: 978-1-893762-17-6
Produced in Sioux Falls, SD by XRX, Inc. 605-338-2450
Printed in the United States of America.

XRX BOOKS
www.knittinguniverse.com

GAUGE
19 sts and 26 rows to 4" over Stockinette Stitch (k on RS, p on WS), using size 4.5mm (US 7) needles

MATERIALS

Plymouth Encore
75% acrylic, 25% wool
3.5oz (100g); 200 yds (180m); 9 wraps/inch
#256 Aran approx 1 per square
Total # of balls 20

Knitting needles
Sizes 5–8 (3.74mm–5mm)
see instructions for details

Tapestry needle

14" pillow forms

Judy Sumner

KNOXVILLE, TENNESSEE

"This Aran square was inspired by a birthday card from my twin granddaughters. The card front had a garden with little cartoon bugs and spiders, and a bunch of X's and O's. When I looked at it I said, 'Kisses and hugs; spiders and bugs.' I had recently charted out a small spider for some socks I was designing and knew immediately what theme I'd use for my square.

"The 'Kisses and Hugs' cable and the 'Leaf Panel' are found in *The Harmony Guide to Aran and Fair Isle Knitting*. The spider and bugs are my own designs.

"I am a retired gerontologist who joined the Knitlist over five years ago. I had knitted in a vacuum for years but the Knitlist inspired me and taught me to try things I had never done before. After my first sock design was published in *Socks, Socks, Socks* (XRX Books), I began designing socks for family and friends. This year, I've sold ten sock patterns and a shawl pattern to yarn companies. My 'retirement' has turned into some of the most fun with knitting I have ever had! My twin granddaughters (almost five) are trying to learn to knit and often provide inspirational names for some of my creations."

Needles Size 4.5mm (US 7)

Extras Cable needle (cn)
Stitch markers

Notes

1 See *School*, p. 60 for ssk, SK2P, S2KP2, and Make 1 knit (M1K), and purl (M1P). **2** Bugs may be placed anywhere on Chart B or Chart D. Plan the placement before beginning charts.

Large Bug Placement

Work body, beg on a WS row Work to bug placement, turn work, cast on 4 sts onto LH needle, k4, turn, p4, turn, bind off 4 sts, turn, sl 1 st to RH needle, work to end of row. Push bug to RS of work. ***Work head on next RS row*** Work to bug body, k into back, front, back of next st, turn, p3, turn, S2KP2, work to end.

Wings *WORK AFTER SQUARE IS COMPLETE* With RS facing, pick up 1 st between bug head and body. *Cast on 4 more sts onto same needle, then bind off 4 sts knitwise, leaving 1 st on needle.* Turn work and rep from * to * for other wing. Pull yarn through bug's body and through st on needle. Fasten off.

Small Bug Placement

Work body, beg on a RS row Work to bug placement, work as for head of large bug.

Wings *WORK AFTER SQUARE IS COMPLETE* Work as for wings of large bug, picking up the first st above bug body, and casting on 3 sts, instead of 4.

Square

Cast on 54 sts. Work 3 ridges, inc 7 sts evenly across last (WS) row—61 sts. ***Beg pats: Row 1*** (RS) K3, work 10 sts Chart A, place marker (pm), 15 sts rev St st (p on RS, k on WS), pm, 20 sts Chart B, pm, 10 sts Chart A, k3. Work 5 more rows in pats as established, keeping first and last 3 sts in garter st (k every row). Work 18 rows in pat, replacing 15 sts rev St st with Chart C. Work 8 rows, replacing Chart C with rev St st. Work 34 rows, replacing 15 sts rev St st with Chart D as foll: Work rows 1–16, then rep rows 13–16 three times more, work rows 17–22—63 sts. ***Next row*** (RS) Knit across all sts, dec 9 sts evenly across—54 sts. Work 3 ridges. Bind off.

Chart A

10 sts

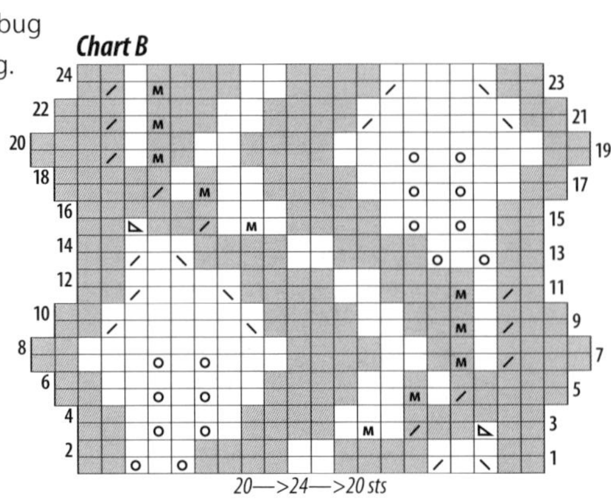

IN OTHER WORDS

MAKE LARGE BOBBLE (MLB)
[K in front and back of st] 3 times, [turn, p6, turn, k6] twice, turn, [p2tog] 3 times, turn, S2KP2.

MAKE SMALL BOBBLE (MSB)
In next st, [k in front and back] twice, [turn, p4, turn, k4] twice, turn, [p2tog] twice, turn, ssk.

1/1 TRPC Sl 1 to cn, hold to back, k1 tbl; p1 from cn.

1/1 TLPC Sl 1 to cn, hold to front, p1; k1 tbl from cn.

2/2 RC Sl 2 to cn, hold to back, k2; k2 from cn.

2/2 LC Sl 2 to cn, hold to front, k2; k2 from cn.

CHART A *OVER 10 STS*
Rows 1, 5, 9, 13 (RS) P1, k8, p1. ***2 and all WS rows*** K1, p8, k1. ***3 and 7*** P1, 2/2 RC, 2/2 LC, p1. ***11 and 15*** P1, 2/2 LC, 2/2 RC, p1. ***16*** Rep row 2. Rep rows 1-16 for Chart A.

CHART B *BEG OVER 20 STS*
Row 1 (RS) P2, ssk, k1, k2tog, p4, k2, p4, yo, k1, yo, p2. ***2*** K2, p3, k4, p2, k4, p3, k2. ***3*** P2, SK2P, p2, p2tog, k1, M1K, k1, p4, k1, [yo, k1] twice, p2. ***4*** K2, p5, k4, p3, k6. ***5*** P4, p2tog, k1, M1P, k2, p4, k2, yo, k1, yo, k2, p2—22 sts. ***6*** K2, p7, k4, p2, k1, p1, k5. ***7*** P3, p2tog, k1, M1P, p1, k2, p4, k3, yo, k1, yo, k3, p2—24 sts. ***8*** K2, p9, k4, p2, k2, p1, k4. ***9*** P2, p2tog, k1, M1P, p2, k2, p4, ssk, k5, k2tog, p2—22 sts. ***10*** K2, p7, k4, p2, k3, p1, k3. ***11*** P1, p2tog, k1, M1P, p3, k2, p4, ssk, k3, k2tog, p2—20 sts. ***12*** K2, p5, k4, p2, k4, p1, k2. ***13*** P2, yo, k1, yo, p4, k2, p4, ssk, k1, k2tog, p2. ***14*** K2, p3, k4, p2, k4, p3, k2. ***15*** P2, k1, [yo, k1] twice, p4, k1, M1K, k1, p2tog, p2, SK2P, p2. ***16*** K6, p3, k4, p5, k2. ***17*** P2, k2, yo, k1, yo, k2, p4, k2, M1P, k1, p2tog, p4—22 sts. ***18*** K5, p1, k1, p2, k4, p7, k2. ***19*** P2, k3, yo, k1, yo, k3, p4, k2, p1, M1P, k1, p2tog, p3—24 sts. ***20*** K4, p1, k2, p2, k4, p9, k2. ***21*** P2, ssk, k5, k2tog, p4, k2, p2, M1P, k1, p2tog, p2—22 sts. ***22*** K3, p1, k3, p2, k4, p7, k2. ***23*** P2, ssk, k3, k2tog, p4, k2, p3, M1P, k1, p2tog, p1—20 sts. ***24*** K2, p1, k4, p2, k4, p5, k2. Rep rows 1-24 for Chart B.

CHART C *OVER 15 STS*
Row 1 (RS) P3, k1 through back loop (tbl), p7, k1 tbl, p3. ***2 and all WS rows*** K the knit sts and p the purl sts tbl. ***3*** P2, k1 tbl, 1/1 TLPC, p5, 1/1 TRPC, k1 tbl, p2. ***5*** P2, [1/1 TLPC] twice, p3, [1/1 TRPC] twice, p2. ***7*** P3, [1/1 TLPC] twice, p1, [1/1 TRPC] twice, p3. ***9*** P4, 1/1 TLPC, k1 tbl, MLB, k1 tbl, 1/1 TRPC, p4. ***11*** P4, 1/1 TRPC, k1 tbl, MSB, k1 tbl, 1/1 TLPC, p4. ***13*** P3, [1/1 TRPC] twice, p1, [1/1 TLPC] twice, p3. ***15*** P2, [1/1 TRPC] twice, p3, [1/1 TLPC] twice, p2. ***17*** P1, [1/1 TRPC] twice, p5, [1/1 TLPC] twice, p1. ***18*** Rep row 2.

CHART D *OVER 15 STS*
Row 1 (RS) [Yo, ssk] twice, p11. ***2*** K11, p4. ***3*** [K2tog, yo] 3 times, p9. ***4*** K9, p6. ***5*** [Yo, ssk] 4 times, p7. ***6*** K7, p8. ***7*** [K2tog, yo] 5 times, p5. ***8*** K5, p10. ***9*** [Yo, ssk] 6 times, p3. ***10*** K3, p12. ***11*** [K2tog, yo] 7 times, p1. ***12*** K1, p14. ***13*** [Yo, ssk] 7 times, p1. ***14 and 16*** Rep row 12. ***15*** Rep row 11. [Rep rows 13–16] 3 times more. ***17*** Rep row 9. ***18*** Rep row 10. ***19*** Rep row 7. ***20*** Rep row 8. ***21*** Rep row 5.

K on RS, p on WS
P on RS, k on WS
Yo
Ssk
K2tog
P2tog
M1K
M1P
K1 tbl on RS, p1 tbl on WS
MSB
MLB
SK2P
1/1 TRPC
1/1 TLPC
2/2 RC
2/2 LC

Chart C

15 sts

Chart D

4-row rep

15 sts

Julie H. Levy

STUART, FLORIDA

"My older sister taught me to knit when I was four and my earliest efforts were sweaters for my dolls. Eventually I graduated to sweaters and hats for friends and myself. When I discovered Elizabeth Zimmermann and Barbara Walker, my knitting life changed completely. I began to design and knitting became even more enjoyable.

"My husband, Howard, and I lived on a boat for 12 years, cruising from the Florida Keys to Cape Cod and back. Many boaters on the Intracoastal Waterway were startled to see the navigator (me) reading the navigational charts while knitting. These days Howard and I have a smaller boat and I still knit while cruising. Along with knitting for our daughter, son-in-law, and three grandchildren, I'm making an evening jacket to wear to our oldest granddaughter's wedding.

"For my square, I used Barbara Walker's Treasury of Knitting Patterns *books. The 'Serpentine Cable' looks like a fisherman's ropes, and 'Aran Diamond and Bobble' is typical Aran patterning. Together they convey the Aran knitting that I want to impart."*

Needles Size 4.5mm (US 7)

Extras Cable needle (cn)

Square

Cast on 48 sts. Work 3 ridges, inc 28 sts evenly across last (RS) row—76 sts. ***Beg Charts A and B: Row 1*** (WS) K3, work 17 sts Chart A, Chart B over 36 sts, 17 sts Chart A, k3. Cont in pats as established, keeping 3 sts each side in garter st (k every row), until 30 rows of Chart A have been worked twice, then work rows 1–15 once more. Work 3 ridges, dec 28 sts evenly across first row—48 sts. Bind off. ∩

Pat Arrangement

3 sts garter st	17 sts Chart A	36 sts Chart B	17 sts Chart A	3 sts garter st

IN OTHER WORDS

MAKE BOBBLE (MB) [(K1, yo) twice, k1] in next st, turn; p5, turn; k5, turn; p2tog, p1, p2tog, turn; sl 1 knitwise, k2tog, psso.
2/1 RPC Sl 1 to cn, hold to back, k2; p1 from cn.
2/1 LPC Sl 2 to cn, hold to front, p1; k2 from cn.
2/2 RC Sl 2 to cn, hold to back, k2; k2 from cn.
2/2 LC Sl 2 to cn, hold to front, k2; k2 from cn.
2/1/2 RPC Sl 3 to cn, hold to back, k2; sl 1 from cn to LH needle and p it; k2 from cn.

CHART A *OVER 17 STS*
Row 1 (WS) K6, p2, k1, p2, k6. ***2*** P6, 2/1/2 RPC, p6. ***3 and all foll WS rows*** K the knit sts and p the purl sts. ***4*** P5, 2/1 RPC, p1, 2/1 LPC, p5. ***6*** P4, 2/1 RPC, p3, 2/1 LPC, p4. ***8*** P4, k2, p2, MB, p2, k2, p4. ***10*** P4, 2/1 LPC, p3, 2/1 RPC, p4. ***12*** P5, 2/1 LPC, p1, 2/1 RPC, p5. ***14*** Rep row 2. ***16*** P5, 2/1 RPC, k1, 2/1 LPC, p5. ***18*** P4, 2/1 RPC, k1, p1, k1, 2/1 LPC, p4. ***20*** P3, 2/1 RPC, [k1, p1] twice, k1, 2/1 LPC, p3. ***22*** P2, 2/1 RPC, [k1, p1] 3 times, k1, 2/1 LPC, p2. ***24*** P2, 2/1 LPC, [p1, k1] 3 times, p1, 2/1 RPC, p2. ***26*** P3, 2/1 LPC, [p1, k1] twice, p1, 2/1 RPC, p3. ***28*** P4, 2/1 LPC, p1, k1, p1, 2/1 RPC, p4. ***30*** Rep row 12. Rep rows 1-30 for Chart A.

CHART B *OVER 36 STS*
Row 1 (WS) K2, p2, [k4, p4] 3 times, k4, p2, k2. ***2*** P2, [2/1 LPC, p2, 2/1 RPC] 4 times, p2. ***3 and all foll WS rows*** K the knit sts and p the purl sts. ***4*** P3, [2/1 LPC, 2/1 RPC, p2] 4 times, p1. ***6*** [P4, 2/2 RC] 4 times, p4. ***8*** P3, [2/1 RPC, 2/1 LPC, p2] 4 times, p1. ***10*** P3, [k2, p2] 8 times, p1. ***12*** Rep row 4. ***14*** Rep row 6. ***16*** Rep row 8. ***18*** P2, 2/1 RPC, p2, [2/1 LPC, 2/1 RPC, p2] 3 times, 2/1 LPC, p2. ***20*** P1, 2/1 RPC, p4, [2/2 LC, p4] 3 times, 2/1 LPC, p1. ***22*** 2/1 RPC, p4, [2/1 RPC, 2/1 LPC, p2] 3 times, p2, 2/1 LPC. ***24*** K2, p5, [k2, p2] 6 times, p3, k2. ***26*** 2/1 LPC, p4, [2/1 LPC, 2/1 RPC, p2] 3 times, p2, 2/1 RPC. ***28*** P1, 2/1 LPC, p4, [2/2 LC, p4] 3 times, 2/1 RPC, p1. Rep rows 1–28 for Chart B.

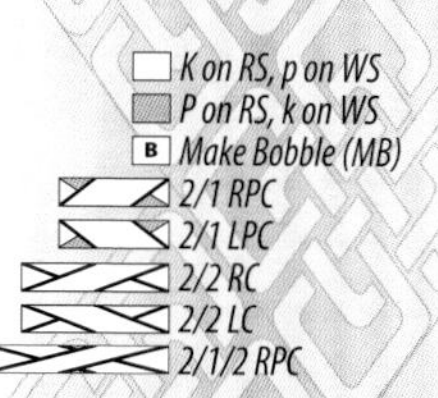

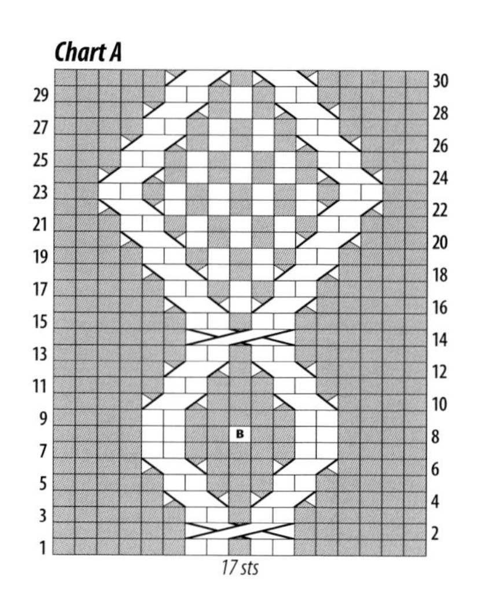

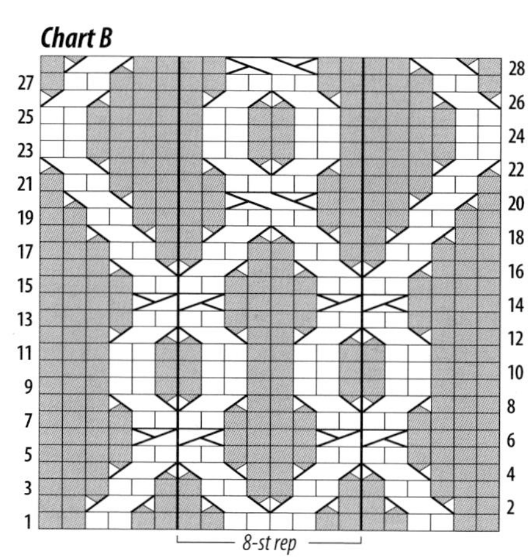

Marian Tabler

CINCINNATI, OHIO

"My mother taught me to knit when I was about 10 years old. I didn't do much knitting after that until I had small children who needed to be kept supplied with hats, mittens, slippers, and sweaters. Over the years I've improved my skills and since retirement, I'm able to devote more time to teaching knitting and experimenting with designing.

"This square, I call 'Tipsy Cable'. I first saw the cable in an '80s pattern book and loved the whimsy of the pattern. The complementary side cables are from Barbara Walker's A Second Treasury of Knitting Patterns.*"*

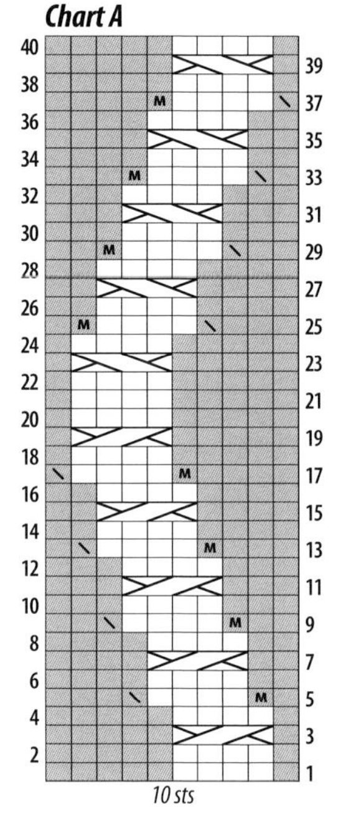

Needles Size 4.5mm (US 7)

Extras Cable needle (cn)
Stitch markers

Note
See *School*, p. 60 for ssp and Make 1 purl (M1P).

Inc 3 [K1, p1] twice in a st.
Dec 3 P2tog, ssp, pass first st over 2nd st.

vSquare
Cast on 61 sts. Work 3 ridges, end with a RS row. ***Foundation row*** (WS) K5, Inc 3, k6, p1 through back loop (tbl), k2, p2, [p1, k1] 3 times, Inc 3, k4, [p1 tbl, k1 tbl] twice, p1 tbl, k4, Inc 3, [k1, p1] 3 times, p2, k2, p1 tbl, k6, Inc 3, k5—73 sts. ***Beg chart pats: Next row*** (RS) K3, p1, place marker (pm), work row 1 of *Chart A over 10 sts*, pm, p1, k1 tbl, p1, pm, work row 1 of Chart B over 15 sts, pm, p2, [k1 tbl, p1 tbl] twice, k1 tbl, p2, pm, work row 1 of Chart C over 15 sts, pm, p1, k1 tbl, p1, pm, work row 21 of Chart A over 10 sts, pm, p1, k3. **2** K4, work row 22 of Chart A over 10 sts, k1, p1 tbl, k1, work row 2 of Chart C over 15 sts, k2, p1 tbl, [k1 tbl, p1 tbl] twice, k2, work row 2 of Chart B over 15 sts, k1, p1 tbl, k1, work row 2 of Chart A over 10 sts, k4. Cont in pats as established until 81 total chart rows have been worked. ***Next row*** (WS) K5, Dec 3, k6, p1 tbl, k2, p3, [k1, p1] twice, k1, Dec 3, k4, [p1 tbl, k1 tbl] twice, p1 tbl, k4, Dec 3, [k1, p1] 3 times, p2, k2, p1 tbl, k6, Dec 3, k5—61 sts. Work 3 ridges. Bind off. ∩

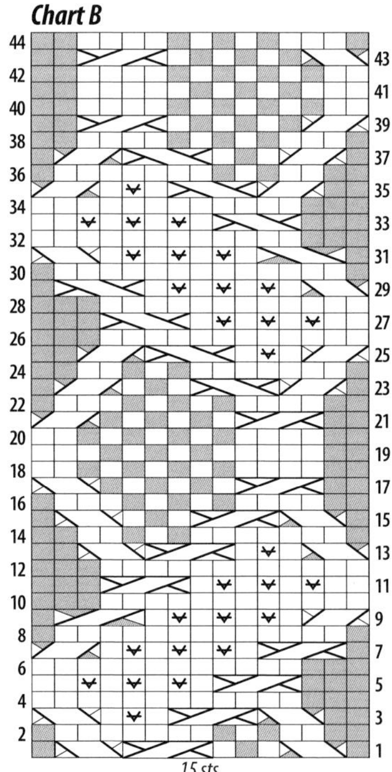

Pat Arrangement

3 sts garter st	1 st rev St st	10 sts Chart A, beg row 21	1 st rev St st	1 st tbl	1 st rev St st	15 sts Chart C, beg row 1	2 sts rev St st	5 sts tbl	2 sts rev St st	15 sts Chart B, beg row 1	1 st rev St st	1 st tbl	1 st rev St st	10 sts Chart A, beg row 1	1 st rev St st	3 sts garter st

center

IN OTHER WORDS

2/1 RC Sl 1 to cn, hold to back, k2; k1 from cn.
2/1 LC Sl 2 to cn, hold to front, k1; k2 from cn.
2/1 RPC Sl 1 to cn, hold to back, k2; p1 from cn.
2/1 LPC Sl 2 to cn, hold to front, p1; k2 from cn.
2/2 RC Sl 2 to cn, hold to back, k2; k2 from cn.
2/2 LC Sl 2 to cn, hold to front, k2; k2 from cn.
2/2 RPC Sl 2 to cn, hold to back, k2; p2 from cn.
2/2 LPC Sl 2 to cn, hold to front, p2; k2 from cn.

CHART A *OVER 10 STS*

Row 1 (RS) P1, k4, p5. ***2 and all WS rows*** K the knit sts and p the purl sts. ***3*** P1, 2/2 RC, p5. ***5*** P1, M1P, k4, ssp, p3. ***7*** P2, 2/2 RC, p4. ***9*** P2, M1P, k4, ssp, p2. ***11*** P3, 2/2 RC, p3. ***13*** P3, M1P, k4, ssp, p1. ***15*** P4, 2/2 RC, p2. ***17*** P4, M1P, k4, ssp. ***19*** P5, 2/2 RC, p1. ***21*** P5, k4, p1. ***23*** P5, 2/2 LC, p1. ***25*** P3, ssp, k4, M1P, p1. ***27*** P4, 2/2 LC, p2. ***29*** P2, ssp, k4, M1P, p2. ***31*** P3, 2/2 LC, p3. ***33*** P1, ssp, k4, M1P, p3. ***35*** P2, 2/2 LC, p4. ***37*** Ssp, k4, M1P, p4. ***39*** P1, 2/2 LC, p5. ***40*** Rep row 2. Rep rows 1-40 for Chart A.

CHART B *OVER 15 STS*

Note Sl sts purlwise with yarn in front.
Row 1 (RS) P1, 2/1 LPC, k1, p1, k1, 2/2 RC, 2/1 LC, p1. ***2*** K1, p7, k1, p1, k1, p2, k2. ***3*** P2, 2/1 LPC, 2/2 RC, k1, sl 1, k1, 2/1 LC. ***4 and 6*** P12, k3. ***5*** P3, 2/2 RC, [k1, sl 1] 3 times, k2. ***7*** P1, 2/2 RC, [k1, sl 1] 3 times, k1, 2/1 RPC. ***8*** K1, p13, k1. ***9*** 2/1 RC, [k1, sl 1] 3 times, k1, 2/2 RPC, p1. ***10 and 12*** K3, p12. ***11*** K2, [sl 1, k1] 3 times, 2/2 RC, p3. ***13*** 2/1 LPC, k1, sl 1, k1, 2/2 RC, 2/1 LC, p2. ***14*** K2, p2, k1, p1, k1, p7, k1. ***15*** P1, 2/1 LPC, 2/2 RC, k1, p1, k1, 2/1 LC, p1. ***16*** K1, p2, [p1, k1] 3 times, p4, k2. ***17*** P2, 2/2 RC, [k1, p1] 3 times, 2/1 LC. ***18 and 20*** P2, [k1, p1] 4 times, p3, k2. ***19*** P2, k5, [p1, k1] 3 times, k2. ***21*** P2, 2/2 RC, [k1, p1] 3 times, 2/1 RPC. ***22*** Rep row 16. ***23*** P1, 2/1 RC, 2/2 LC, k1, p1, k1, 2/1 RPC, p1. ***24*** Rep row 14. ***25*** 2/1 RC, k1, sl 1, k1, 2/2 LC, 2/1 RPC, p2. ***26 and 28*** Rep row 10. ***27*** K2, [sl 1, k1] 3 times, 2/2 LC, p3. ***29*** 2/1 LPC, [k1, sl 1] 3 times, k1, 2/2 LC, p1. ***30*** Rep row 8. ***31*** P1, 2/2 LPC, [k1, sl 1] 3 times, k1, 2/1 LC. ***32 and 34*** Rep row 4. ***33*** P3, 2/2 LC, [k1, sl 1] 3 times, k2. ***35*** P2, 2/1 RC, 2/2 LC, k1, sl 1, k1, 2/1 RPC. ***36*** Rep row 2. ***37*** P1, 2/1 RC, k1, p1, k1, 2/2 LC, 2/1 RPC, p1. ***38*** K2, p4, [k1, p1] 3 times, p2, k1. ***39*** 2/1 RC, [p1, k1] 3 times, 2/2 RC, p2. ***40 and 42*** K2, p4, [k1, p1] 4 times, p1. ***41*** K3, [p1, k1] 3 times, k4, p2. ***43*** 2/1 LPC, [p1, k1] 3 times, 2/2 RC, p2. ***44*** K2, p4, [k1, p1] 3 times, p2, k1. Rep rows 1-44 for Chart B.

CHART C *OVER 15 STS*

Rows 1–16 Work rows 23–38 of Chart B. ***17–22*** Work rows 39–44 of Chart B, except work 2/2 LC, instead of 2/2 RC. ***23–38*** Work rows 1–16 of Chart B. ***39–44*** Work rows 17–22 of Chart B, except work 2/2 LC, instead of 2/2 RC. Rep rows 1–44 for Chart C.

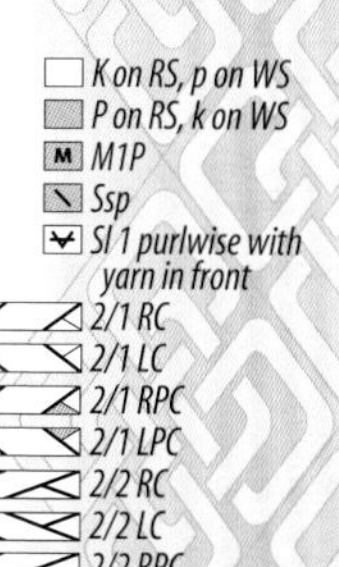

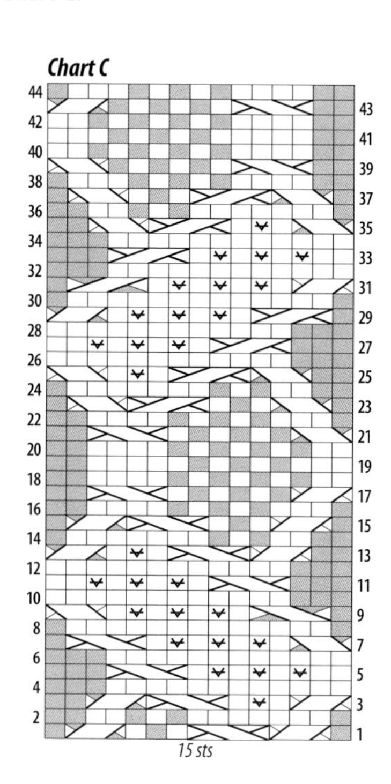

Meredith K. Morioka

GARDEN CITY, KANSAS

"When I saw the announcement of the Aran Afghan Square contest, I thought I knew exactly what I would submit—a square based on the Aran tunic I designed and am currently knitting for myself from some of my handspun yarn.

"However, once I began to fiddle with ideas I kept thinking, 'Yarn over, yarn over.' This was probably because I'm also knitting a Faroese shawl with another of my handspun yarns. At this point I remembered that Gladys Thompson, in her book, Patterns for Guernseys, Jerseys, and Arans, *presents several Aran sweaters with openwork patterns.*

"The center lattice pattern is from The Arco Guide to Knitting Stitches *(Arco, 1985). The half-diamond pattern I 'unvented' to fit my stitch and row requirements after digesting similar zigzag patterns from Thompson's book.*

"The finished product pleases me so much that I think my next sweater project will be based on the newly designed square."

Needles Size 3.75mm (US 5)

Extras Cable needle (cn)

Note

See *School*, p. 60 for SKP.

Square

Cast on 60 sts. Work 3 ridges, inc 3 sts on last (RS) row—63 sts. ***Foundation row*** (WS) K5, [p1, k1] 5 times, k1, p3, k9, p3, k1, p3, k9, p3, k3, [p1, k1] 5 times, k3. ***Beg Charts A and B: Next row*** (RS) K3, work row 1 of Chart A over 12 sts, row 1 of Chart B over 33 sts, row 21 of Chart A over 12 sts, k3. ***Next row*** K3, then reading charts from left to right, work row 22 of Chart A over 12 sts, row 2 of Chart B over 33 sts, row 2 of Chart A over 12 sts, k3. Cont in pats as established until 20 rows of Chart B have been worked 5 times. ***Next row*** (RS) Knit, dec 3 sts evenly across—60 sts. Work 3 ridges. Bind off. ∩

Pat Arrangement

3 sts garter st	12 sts Chart A, beg row 21	33 sts Chart B, beg row 1	12 sts Chart A, beg row 1	3 sts garter st

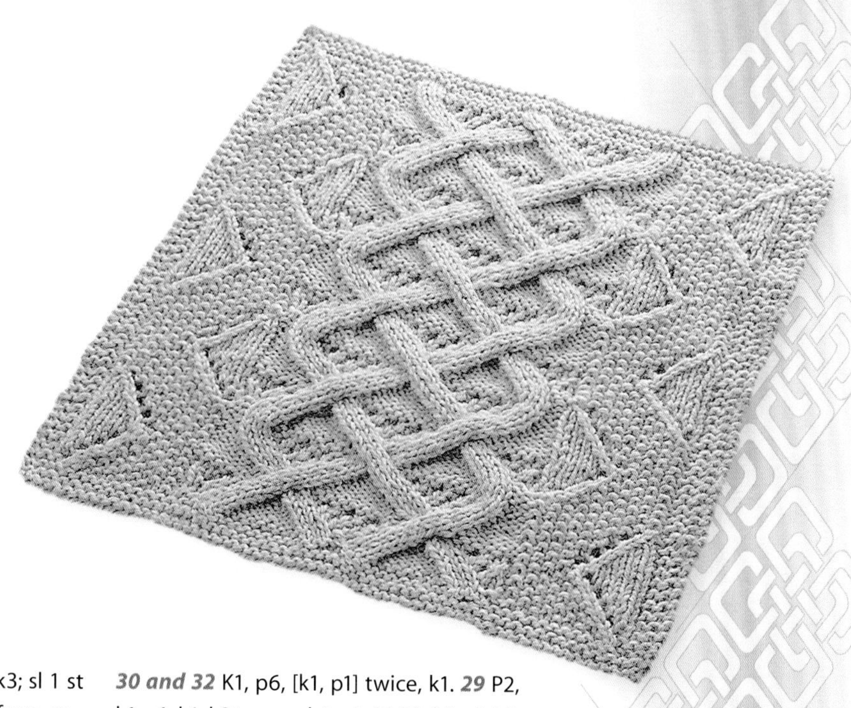

IN OTHER WORDS

3/1/3 RPC Sl 4 to cn, hold to back, k3; sl 1 st from cn to LH needle and p it; k3 from cn.
3/1/3 LPC Sl 4 to cn, hold to front, k3; sl 1 st from cn to LH needle and p it; k3 from cn.

CHART A *OVER 12 STS*
Row 1 (RS) P1, yo, SKP, [p1, k1] 4 times, p1. ***2 and 4*** K2, [p1, k1] 3 times, p3, k1. ***3*** P1, k1, yo, SKP, [k1, p1] 4 times. ***5*** P1, k2, yo, SKP, [p1, k1] 3 times, p1. ***6 and 8*** K2, [p1, k1] twice, p5, k1. ***7*** P1, k3, yo, SKP, [k1, p1] 3 times. ***9*** P1, k4, yo, SKP, [p1, k1] twice, p1. ***10*** K2, p1, k1, p7, k1. ***11*** P1, k4, k2tog, yo, [p1, k1] twice, p1. ***12 and 14*** Rep row 6. ***13*** P1, k3, k2tog, yo, [k1, p1] 3 times. ***15*** P1, k2, k2tog, yo, [p1, k1] 3 times, p1. ***16 and 18*** Rep row 2. ***17*** P1, k1, k2tog, yo, [k1, p1] 4 times. ***19*** P1, k2tog, yo, [p1, k1] 4 times, p1. ***20*** K2, [p1, k1] 5 times. ***21*** P2, [k1, p1] 3 times, k1, k2tog, yo, p1. ***22*** K1, p2, [k1, p1] 4 times, k1. ***23*** P2, [k1, p1] 3 times, k2tog, yo, k1, p1. ***24 and 26*** K1, p4, [k1, p1] 3 times, k1. ***25*** P2, [k1, p1] twice, k1, k2tog, yo, k2, p1. ***27*** P2, [k1, p1] twice, k2tog, yo, k3, p1. ***28, 30 and 32*** K1, p6, [k1, p1] twice, k1. ***29*** P2, k1, p1, k1, k2tog, yo, k4, p1. ***31*** P2, k1, p1, k1, yo, SKP, k4, p1. ***33*** P2, [k1, p1] twice, yo, SKP, k3, p1. ***34 and 36*** Rep row 24. ***35*** P2, [k1, p1] twice, k1, yo, SKP, k2, p1. ***37*** P2, [k1, p1] 3 times, yo, SKP, k1, p1. ***38*** Rep row 22. ***39*** P2, [k1, p1] 3 times, k1, yo, SKP, p1. ***40*** Rep row 20. Rep rows 1–40 for Chart A.

CHART B *OVER 33 STS*
Row 1 (RS) K1, [yo, k2, SKP, p7, k2tog, k2, yo, k1] twice. ***2*** [P5, k7, p4] twice, p1. ***3*** K2, yo, k2, SKP, p5, k2tog, k2, yo, k2tog, yo, k1, yo, k2, SKP, p5, k2tog, k2, yo, k2. ***4*** [P6, k5, p5] twice, p1. ***5*** [K2tog, yo, k1, yo, k2, SKP, p3, k2tog, k2, yo, k2tog, yo] twice, k1. ***6*** [P7, k3, p6] twice, p1. ***7*** K1, k2tog, yo, k1, yo, k2, SKP, p1, k2tog, k2, [yo, k2tog] 3 times, yo, k1, yo, k2, SKP, p1, k2tog, k2, yo, k2tog, yo, k2. ***8*** [P8, k1, p7] twice, p1. ***9*** [P5, 3/1/3 RPC, p4] twice, p1. ***10*** [K5, p3, k1, p3, k4] twice, k1. ***11*** [P4, k2tog, k2, yo, k1, yo, k2, SKP, p3] twice, p1. ***12*** [K4, p9, k3] twice, k1. ***13*** [P3, k2tog, k2, yo, k2tog, yo, k1, yo, k2, SKP, p2] twice, p1. ***14*** [K3, p11, k2] twice, k1. ***15*** [P2, k2tog, k2, (yo, k2tog) twice, yo, k1, yo, k2, SKP, p1] twice, p1. ***16*** [K2, p13, k1] twice, k1. ***17*** [P1, k2tog, k2, (yo, k2tog) 3 times, yo, k1, yo, k2, SKP] twice, p1. ***18*** [K1, p15] twice, k1. ***19*** P1, k3, p9, 3/1/3 LPC, p9, k3, p1. ***20*** [K1, p3, k9, p3] twice, k1. Rep rows 1–20 for Chart B.

Chart A

12 sts

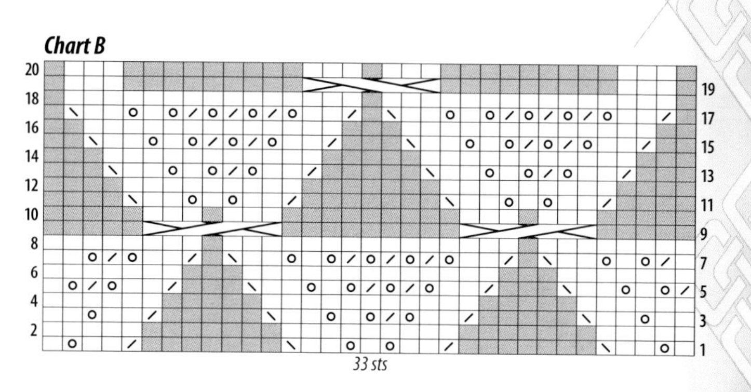

Kathleen T. Carty

KANATA, ONTARIO, CANADA

"My mother taught me basic knitting stitches when I was about 7 years old and my grandmother taught me to knit mittens a couple of years later. The rest of my knitting skills I've learned from reading patterns, books, and magazines. I've been an avid knitter since my teens and have enjoyed trying out new techniques. I value publications such as Knitter's *to keep me in touch with trends that others are developing and to continue my education. Knitter's has also been instrumental in encouraging me to develop my own patterns.*

"When I saw Julie Hoff-Weisenberger's oak leaf pattern (Fall '96 K44), I decided to use it in an afghan. I alternated vertical rows of oak leaf pattern, leaf vine (from Deborah Newton's Secret Garden in Summer '95 K39), and trellis stitch. My sister saw the result and fell in love with the pattern. She asked me to make her an afghan with the oak leaf pattern around the edge and a textured pattern in the middle. The method I used for her afghan is the one I used for my square. The challenge was to find a cable that turned the corner with eye appeal, that had an even number of repeats along the 12" side, and that had three consecutive rows without crossed stitches so that the grafting didn't involve crossed stitches."

Needles Size 4.5mm (US 7); Set of five size 4.5mm (US 7) double-pointed needles (dpn)

Extras Cable needle (cn); Crochet hook

Pat Arrangement

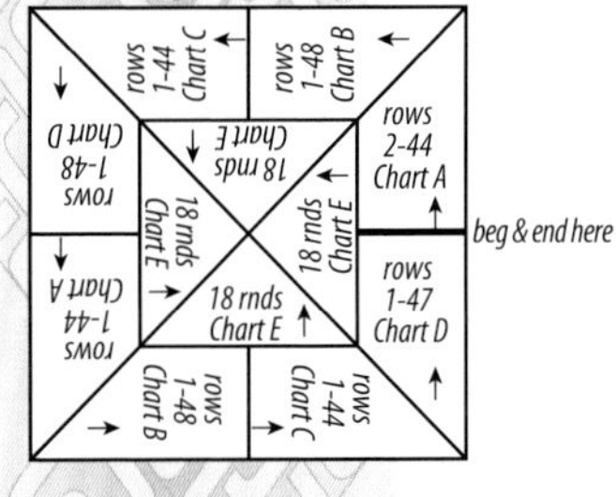

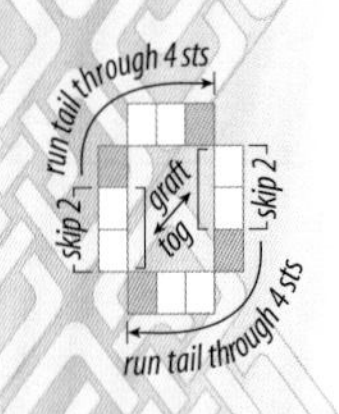

Notes

1 See *School*, p. 60 for chain cast-on, St st grafting, and ssp. ***2*** Work cable border first, then the center section.

Cable Border

Chain cast on 19 sts (counts as row 1 of Chart A). *Work rows 2–44 of Chart A, rows 1–48 of Chart B, rows 1–44 of Chart C, rows 1–48 of Chart D; rep from* once more beg with row 1 of Chart A, and end with row 47 of Chart D. Cut yarn, leaving a 20" tail. Graft open sts to chain cast-on sts, removing chain first (see illustration on p. 58).

Center Section

With RS facing and dpn, pick up and k29 sts along one inside edge of square; rep from 3 times more—116 sts divided evenly over 4 dpns. Join and bind off all sts. With dpn, beg at first bound-off st and pick up and k 1 st in back purl bump of each st around—116 sts divided evenly over 4 dpns. Join and work 18 rnds of Chart E over each dpn—12 sts. Cut yarn, leaving tail. [Skip 2 sts, run tail through 4 sts] twice (see illustration, left), pull tog and tighten. Graft rem 4 sts tog over tightened circle, using St st grafting. ∩

IN OTHER WORDS

1/1 RC Skip first st on LH needle and k 2nd st, then k first st, sl both sts off needle.
1/1 LC With RH needle behind work, k 2nd st on LH needle through back lp, then k first st through front lp, sl both sts off needle.
2/1 RPC Sl 1 to cn, hold to back, k2; p1 from cn.
2/1 LPC Sl 2 to cn, hold to front, p1; k2 from cn.
2/2 RC Sl 2 to cn, hold to back, k2; k2 from cn.
2/2 LC Sl 2 to cn, hold to front, k2; k2 from cn.
WRAP ST & TURN (W&T) With yarn in back, sl 1 purlwise, bring yarn to front and sl st back to LH needle (1 st wrapped). Turn work.
HIDE KNIT WRAPS (HKW) K 2 wraps tog with st on LH needle.
HIDE PURL WRAPS (HPW) P st on LH needle tog with 2 wraps.
1/1 HWRC (Worked on row 7 of Chart B only) Sl 1 st with 2 wraps to cn, hold to back, k1; k st and wraps tog from cn.

CHART A *WORKED OVER 19 STS TO 1 ST*
Row 1 (RS) K5, p3, k4, p3, k2, p2. ***2*** (WS) K2, p2, k3, p4, k3, p2, k3. ***3*** K3, 1/1 RC, p3, 2/2 RC, p3, 1/1 LC, p2. ***4 and all foll WS rows (except 40, 42 and 44)*** K the knit sts and p the purl sts to last 3 sts, k3. ***5*** K5, p2, 2/1 RPC, 2/1 LPC, p2, k2, p2. ***7*** K3, 1/1 RC, p1, 2/1 RPC, p2, 2/1 LPC, p1, 1/1 LC, p2. ***9*** K5, p1, k2, p4, k2, p1, k2, p2. ***11*** K3, 1/1 RC, p1, 2/1 LPC, p2, 2/1 RPC, p1, 1/1 LC, p2. ***13*** K5, p2, 2/1 LPC,

2/1 RPC, p2, k2, p2. ***15*** Rep row 3. ***17*** Rep row 1. ***19*** K3, 1/1 RC, p3, 2/2 RC, p3, 1/1 LC, W&T. ***21*** K5, p2, 2/1 RPC, 2/1 LPC, p2, W&T. ***23*** K3, 1/1 RC, p1, 2/1 RPC, p2, 2/1 LPC, W&T. ***25*** K5, p1, k2, p4, k1, W&T. ***27*** K3, 1/1 RC, p1, k2, p3, W&T. ***29*** K5, p1, k2, p2, W&T. ***31*** K3, 1/1 RC, p1, k2, p1, W&T. ***33*** K5, p1, k1, W&T. ***35*** K3, 1/1 RC, p1, W&T. ***37*** K5, W&T. ***39*** K3, W&T. ***40*** K3. ***41*** K2, W&T. ***42*** K2. ***43*** K1, W&T. ***44*** K1.

CHART B *WORKED OVER 2 STS TO 19 STS*

Row 1 (RS) K1, W&T. ***2*** K1. ***3*** K1, HKW, W&T. ***4*** K2. ***5*** K2, HKW, W&T. ***6*** K3. ***7*** K3, 1/1 HWRC, W&T. ***8 and all foll WS rows*** K the knit sts and p the purl sts to last 3 sts, k3. ***9*** K5, HPW, W&T. ***11*** K3, 1/1 RC, p1, HKW, W&T. ***13*** K5, p1, k1, HKW, p1, W&T. ***15*** K3, 1/1 RC, p1, k2, p1, HPW, W&T. ***17*** K5, p1, k2, p2, HPW, W&T. ***19*** K3, 1/1 RC, p1, k2, p3, HPW, k1, W&T. ***21*** K5, p1, k2, p4, k1, HKW, W&T. ***23*** K3, 1/1 RC, p1, k2, p4, k2, HPW, W&T. ***25*** K5, p1, k2, p4, k2, p1, HKW, k1, W&T. ***27*** K3, 1/1 RC, p1, 2/1 LPC, p2, 2/1 RPC, p1, 1/1 LC, HPW, p1. ***29*** K5, p2, 2/1 LPC, 2/1 RPC, p2, k2, p2. ***31*** K3, 1/1 RC, p3, 2/2 LC, p3, 1/1 LC, p2. ***33*** K5, p3, k4, p3, k2, p2. ***35*** Rep row 31. ***37*** K5, p2, 2/1 RPC, 2/1 LPC, p2, k2, p2. ***39*** K3, 1/1 RC, p1, 2/1 RPC, p2, 2/1 LPC, p1, 1/1 LC, p2. ***41*** K5, p1, k2, p4, k2, p1, k2, p2. ***43*** K3, 1/1 RC, p1, 2/1 LPC, p2, 2/1 RPC, p1, 1/1 LC, p2. ***45*** Rep row 29. ***47*** Rep row 31. ***48*** Rep row 8.

CHART E *OVER 116 STS, DEC'D TO 12 STS*

(***Note*** Rep instructions 4 times for each rnd.) ***Rnd 1*** 1/1 RC, ssp, [k1, p1] 11 times, k1, p2tog. ***2*** K2, ssp, [p1, k1] 10 times, p1, p2tog. ***3*** K2, [p1, k1] 11 times, p1. ***4*** K2, ssp, [p1, k1] 9 times, p1, p2tog. ***5*** 1/1 RC, ssp, [p1, k1] 8 times, p1, p2tog. ***6*** K2, p2, [k1, p1] 8 times, p1. ***7*** K2, ssp, [p1, k1] 7 times, p1, p2tog. ***8*** K2, ssp, [k1, p1] 6 times, k1, p2tog. ***9*** 1/1 RC, p2, [k1, p1] 6 times, p1. ***10*** K2, ssp, [k1, p1] 5 times, k1, p2tog. ***11*** K2, ssp, [k1, p1] 4 times, k1, p2tog. ***12*** K2, [p1, k1] 5 times, p1. ***13*** 1/1 RC, ssp, [k1, p1] 3 times, k1, p2tog. ***14*** K2, ssp, [p1, k1] twice, p1, p2tog. ***15*** K2, [p1, k1] 3 times, p1. ***16*** K2, ssp, p1, k1, p1, p2tog. ***17*** 1/1 RC, ssp, p1, p2tog. ***18*** K2, p3tog.

Charts C and D continue on p. 58 along with grafting illustration.

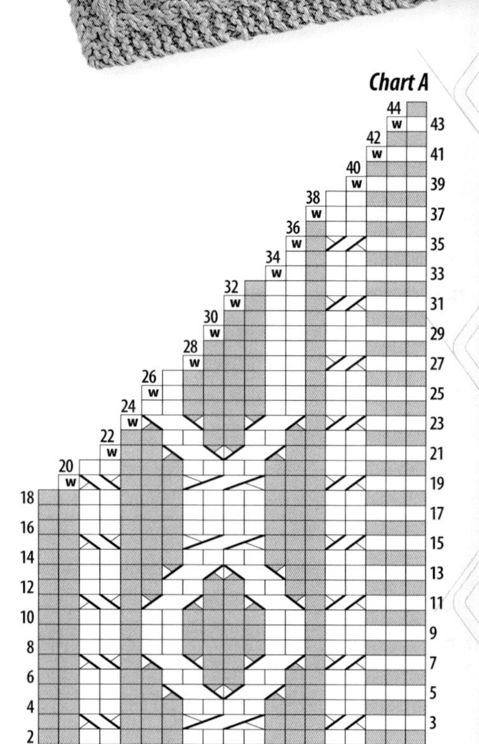

Chart B
19 sts

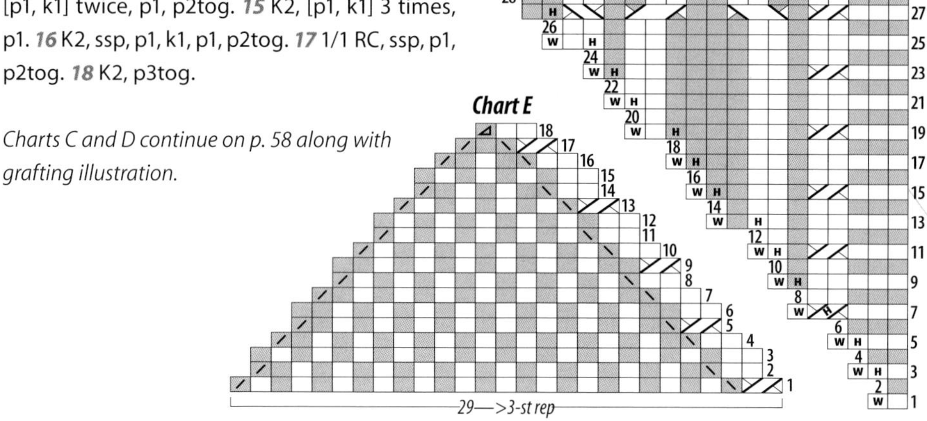

Vicki Sever

OSHKOSH, WISCONSIN

"How I learned to knit is somewhat of a mystery. I imagine someone showed me the basics when I was young, however, I don't have any recollection of this experience. I taught myself the finer points of knitting through books and magazines, and learned to design by creating countless sweaters for my special niece and nephew.

"The loss of my sister to breast cancer in December 1999 was the inspiration for this square. Each motif in the square represents a different symbol. The ribbon, which is shown in the same aran color as the rest of the square, I've also knit in pink for the symbol of the fight against breast cancer; the cross stands for faith; the anchor stands for hope; and naturally, the heart is for love.

"Faith, hope, and love are my wish for everyone—especially those whose lives have been touched by breast cancer."

Needles Size 4mm (US 6)

Extras Cable needle (cn)
Stitch markers

INC 2

K on RS, p on WS
P on RS, k on WS
K2tog
Ssk
SK2P
K3tog
Make 1 (M1)
Make Bobble (MB)
Inc 2 on RS
Inc 2 on WS
1/2 RPC
1/2 LPC
2/1 RPC
2/1 LPC
2/2 RPC
2/2 LPC
2/2 KPRC
2/2 PKLC
3/1 RC
3/1 LC
3/1 RPC
3/1 LPC
3/2 KPRC
3/2 PKLC
2/1/2 RPC
2/1/2 LPC
3/1/3 RC
Dec 4
Dec 6

Note

See *School*, p. 60 for M1, ssk and SK2P.

Moss st

Row 1 (RS) *P1, k1; rep from*. ***2 and 4*** K the knit sts and p the purl sts. ***3*** K the purl sts and p the knit sts. Rep rows 3 and 4 for Moss st.

Square

Cast on 57 sts. Work 3 ridges, ending with a RS row. ***Next row*** Knit. ***Next row*** (RS) K3, p to last 3 sts, k3. ***Next row*** Knit. ***Beg Charts A, B, and C: Row 1*** (RS) K3, p3, place marker (pm), work Chart A over 13 sts, pm, p3, pm, Chart B over 13 sts, pm, p3, pm, Chart C over 13 sts, pm, p3, k3—65 sts. ***2*** K6, then reading charts from left to right, work 15 sts Chart C, k3, 17 sts Chart B, k3, 15 sts Chart A, k6—71 sts. Cont in pats as established through chart row 24—57 sts. Remove markers. ***Beg Charts D and B: Row 1*** (RS) K3, work 9 sts in Moss st, pm, work Chart D over 13 sts, pm, work 10 sts in Moss st, pm, p3, pm, work Chart B over 13 sts, pm, p3, k3—61 sts. Cont in pats as established through chart row 24—63 sts. Cont working pats as established, except work Chart A in place of Chart B, until 48 rows of Chart D have been worked—57 sts. Work 3 ridges. Bind off. ∩

IN OTHER WORDS

MAKE BOBBLE (MB) [(K1, p1) twice, k1] into a st, sl 2nd, 3rd, 4th, and 5th st, one at a time, over first st.

INC 2 (ON RS) K into back and front of a st, then insert LH needle into the vertical strand that runs between the 2 sts just made and k into back of this strand (see illustration, left). **INC 2 (ON WS)** [P1, yo, p1] into a st.

DEC 4 Sl 3 knitwise, one at a time, to RH needle, *pass 2nd st on RH needle over first (center) st; sl center st back to LH needle, pass 2nd st on LH needle over it*, sl center st back to RH needle, work from * to * once more, p center st.

DEC 6 Sl 4 knitwise, one at a time, to RH needle, *pass 2nd st on RH needle over first (center) st; sl center st back to LH needle, pass 2nd st on LH needle over it*, sl center st back to RH needle**, work from * to ** once more, then from * to * once, k center st.

1/2 RPC Sl 2 to cn, hold to back, k1; p2 from cn.
1/2 LPC Sl 1 to cn, hold to front, p2; k1 from cn.
2/1 RPC Sl 1 to cn, hold to back, k2; p1 from cn.
2/1 LPC Sl 2 to cn, hold to front, p1; k2 from cn.
2/2 RPC Sl 2 to cn, hold to back, k2; p2 from cn.
2/2 LPC Sl 2 to cn, hold to front, p2; k2 from cn.
2/2 KPRC Sl 2 to cn, hold to back, k2; [k1, p1] from cn.
2/2 PKLC Sl 2 to cn, hold to front, p1, k1; k2 from cn.
3/1 RC Sl 1 to cn, hold to back, k3; k1 from cn.
3/1 LC Sl 3 to cn, hold to front, k1; k3 from cn.
3/1 RPC Sl 1 to cn, hold to back, k3; p1 from cn.
3/1 LPC Sl 3 to cn, hold to front, p1; k3 from cn.
3/2 KPRC Sl 2 to cn, hold to back, k3; [k1, p1] from cn.
3/2 PKLC Sl 3 to cn, hold to front, p1, k1; k3 from cn.
2/1/2 RPC Sl 3 to cn, hold to back, k2; sl last st from cn to LH needle and p it; k2 from cn.
2/1/2 LPC Sl 3 to cn, hold to front, k2; sl last st from cn to LH needle and p it; k2 from cn.
3/1/3 RC Sl 4 to cn, hold to back, k3; sl last st from cn to LH needle and k it; k3 from cn.

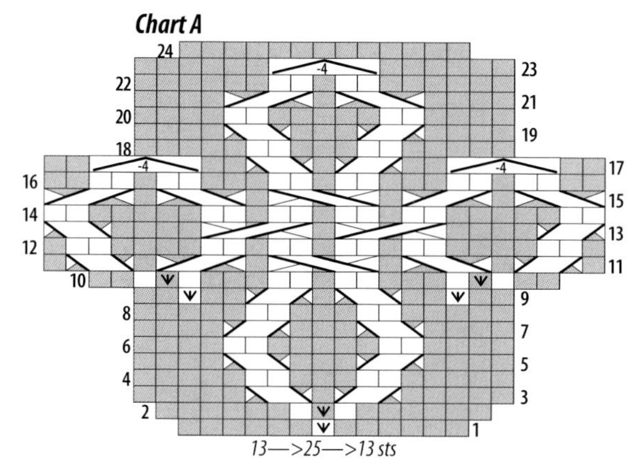

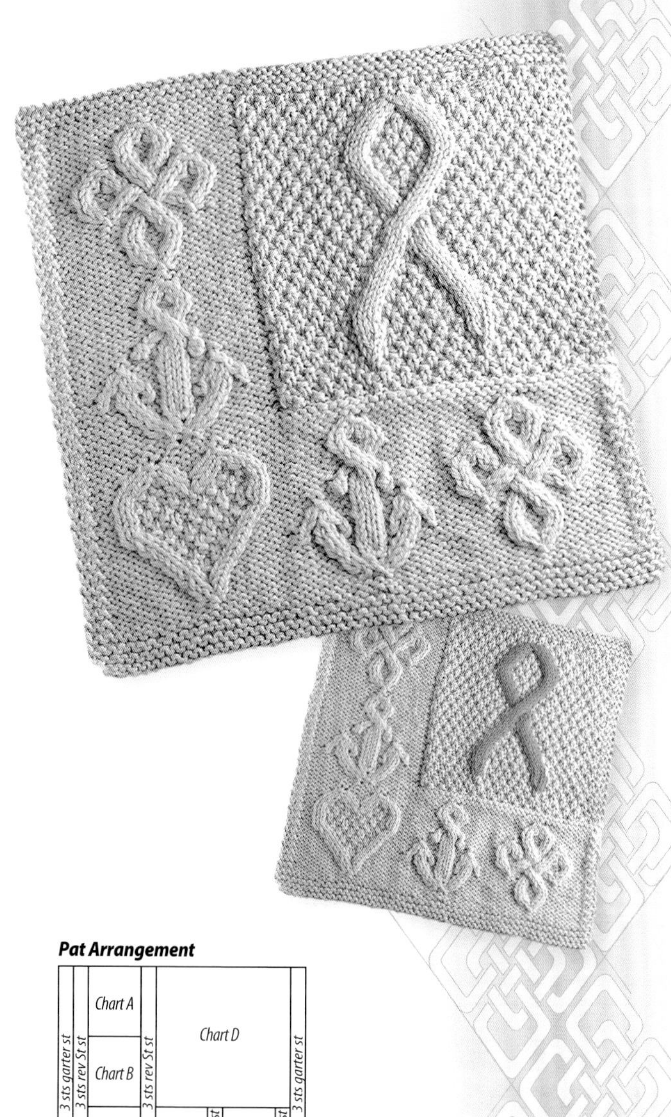

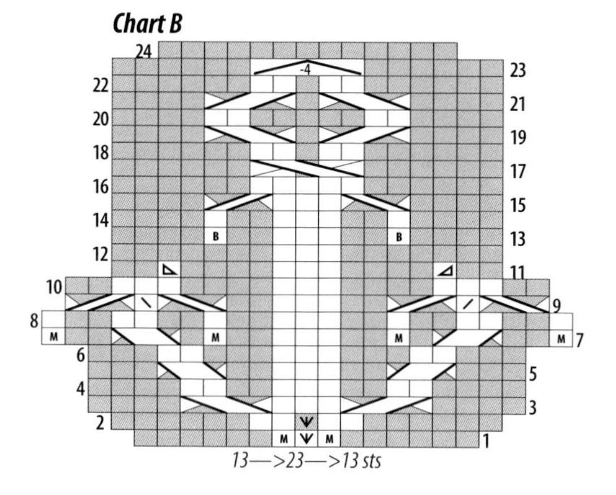

Pat Arrangement

3 sts garter st	3 sts rev St st	Chart A / Chart B / Chart C	3 sts rev St st	Chart D / Chart B, 3 sts rev St st, Chart A, 3 sts rev St st	3 sts garter st

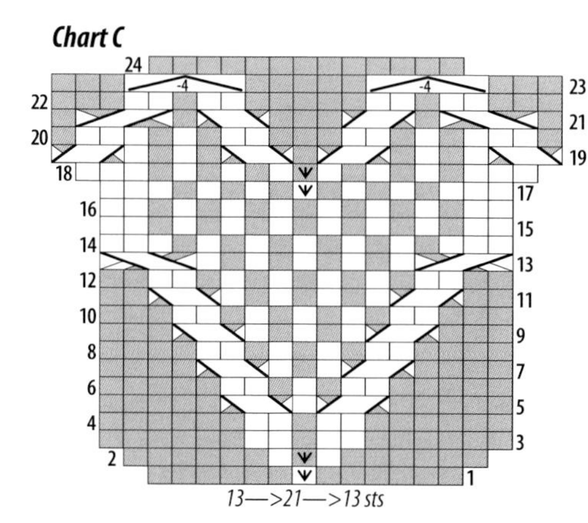

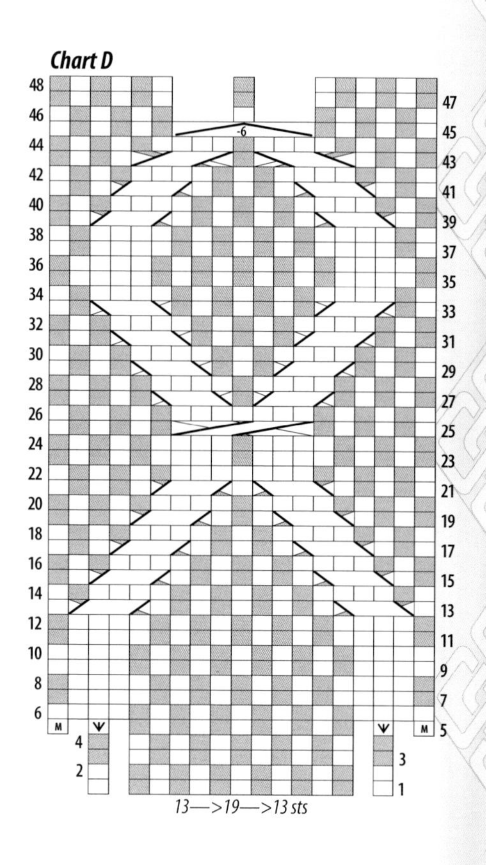

CHART A *OVER 13 TO 25 TO 13 STS*

Row 1 (RS) P6, Inc 2, p6—15 sts. ***2*** (WS) K6, p1, Inc 2, p1, k6—17 sts. ***3*** P5, 2/1 RPC, p1, 2/1 LPC, p5. ***4*** K5, p2, k3, p2, k5. ***5*** P4, 2/1 RPC, p3, 2/1 LPC, p4. ***6*** K4, p2, k5, p2, k4. ***7*** P4, 2/1 LPC, p3, 2/1 RPC, p4. ***8*** Rep row 4. ***9*** P2, Inc 2, p2, 2/1 LPC, p1, 2/1 RPC, p2, Inc 2, p2—21 sts. ***10*** K2, p1, Inc 2, p1, k3, p2, k1, p2, k3, p1, Inc 2, p1, k2—25 sts. ***11*** P1, 2/1 RPC, p1, 2/2 LPC, p1, 2/1/2 LPC, p1, 2/2 RPC, p1, 2/1 LPC, p1. ***12*** *K1, p2, k4, p2, k1*, p2, k1, p2, rep from * to * once. ***13*** 2/1 RPC, p4, 2/1/2 RPC, p1, 2/1/2 RPC, p4, 2/1 LPC. ***14*** P2, k5, p2, [k1, p2] 3 times, k5, p2. ***15*** 2/2 LPC, p1, 2/2 RPC, p1, 2/1/2 LPC, p1, 2/2 LPC, p1, 2/2 RPC. ***16*** K2, p2, k1, p2, [k3, p2, k1, p2] twice, k2. ***17*** P2, Dec 4, p2, 2/1 RPC, p1, 2/1 LPC, p2, Dec 4, p2—17 sts. ***18-20*** Rep rows 4-6. ***21*** P4, 2/2 LPC, p1, 2/2 RPC, p4. ***22*** K6, p2, k1, p2, k6. ***23*** P6, Dec 4, p6—13 sts. ***24*** Knit.
(continues on p. 56)

Ginette Belanger

ST. LAURENT, QUEBEC, CANADA

"I'm a French Canadian and I live in Montreal, Quebec. I was taught to knit in Catholic school when I was 10 years old. When I was 20, I learned English as a second language. I love your magazine and find it inspiring. I have been designing my knit garments for many years and it was a nice challenge to participate in your contest. I really enjoyed the experience of creating this afghan square.

"I was inspired when I first started the Master Knitter's Program with the Canadian Knitting Guild. We had to design different patterns and that is when my creativity began to flow and I started to try new techniques. It was fun to knit this square and I hope that everyone will enjoy it as much as I did."

Needles Size 4mm (US 6)

Extras Cable needle (cn)

Square

Cast on 48 sts. Work 3 ridges, inc 24 sts evenly across last (WS) row—72 sts. ***Beg Charts A and B: Row 1*** (RS) K3, work Chart A over 22 sts, work 22 sts of Chart B, work Chart A over 22 sts, k3. Keeping first and last 3 sts in garter st (k every row), cont in chart pats as established over center 66 sts until 24 rows of Chart B have been worked 3 times, then work rows 1–4 once more. ***Next row*** (RS) Knit, dec 24 sts evenly across—48 sts. Work 3 ridges. Bind off. ∩

IN OTHER WORDS

INC 2 [K1, p1, k1] into a st.
2/1 RPC Sl 1 to cn, hold to back, k2; p1 from cn.
2/1 LPC Sl 2 to cn, hold to front, p1; k2 from cn.
2/2 RC Sl 2 to cn, hold to back, k2; k2 from cn.
2/2 LC Sl 2 to cn, hold to front, k2; k2 from cn.
2/2 RPC Sl 2 to cn, hold to back, k2; p2 from cn.
2/2 LPC Sl 2 to cn, hold to front, p2; k2 from cn.

- *K on RS, p on WS*
- *P on RS, k on WS*
- *Inc 2*
- *P3tog*
- *2/1 RPC*
- *2/1 LPC*
- *2/2 RC*
- *2/2 LC*
- *2/2 RPC*
- *2/2 LPC*

CHART A *MULTIPLE OF 4 STS, PLUS 2*
Rows 1 and 3 (RS) Purl. ***2*** K1, *Inc 2, p3tog; rep from*, end k1. ***4*** K1, *p3tog, Inc 2; rep from*, end k1. Rep rows 1–4 for Chart A.

Chart A

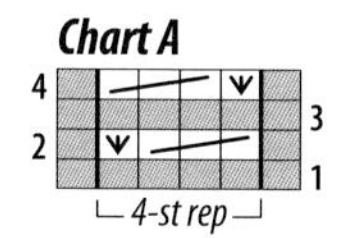

CHART B *OVER 22 STS*
Row 1 (RS) P6, 2/2 RC, k2, 2/2 LC, p6. ***2 and all WS rows*** K the knit sts and p the purl sts. ***3*** P4, 2/2 RPC, k2, 2/2 RC, 2/2 LPC, p4. ***5*** P2, 2/2 RPC, p1, 2/1 RPC, k2, 2/1 LPC, p1, 2/2 LPC, p2. ***7*** 2/2 RPC, p2, 2/1 RPC, p1, k2, p1, 2/1 LPC, p2, 2/2 LPC. ***9*** K2, p3, 2/1 RPC, p2, k2, p2, 2/1 LPC, p3, k2. ***11*** 2/2 LPC, 2/1 RPC, p3, k2, p3, 2/1 LPC, 2/2 RPC. ***13*** P2, 2/2 RC, p4, k2, p4, 2/2 LC, p2. ***15*** 2/2 RPC, 2/2 LPC, p2, k2, p2, 2/2 RPC, 2/2 LPC. ***17*** K2, p4, 2/2 LPC, k2, 2/2 RPC, p4, k2. ***19*** 2/2 LPC, p4, 2/2 LC, k2, p4, 2/2 RPC. ***21*** P2, 2/2 LPC, p2, k2, 2/2 RC, p2, 2/2 RPC, p2. ***23*** P4, 2/2 LPC, 2/2 LC, k2, 2/2 RPC, p4. ***24*** Rep row 2. Rep rows 1–24 for Chart B.

Chart B

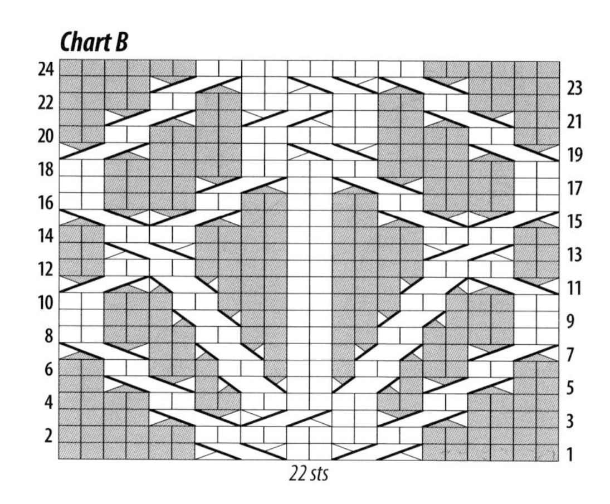

Pat Arrangement

3 sts garter st	22 sts Chart A	22 sts Chart B	22 sts Chart A	3 sts garter st

Barbara Selesnick

OXNARD, CALIFORNIA

"I have been a flight attendant for Continental Airlines for 23 years. It has been an interesting job that takes me to many different places. My favorite part of the day is talking to the passengers–I have met some wonderful people over the years. Early in my career, I developed one particular pastime that has given me so many wonderful moments. Whenever I see someone wearing a locket, I always inquire what treasures are inside the locket. Many show me pictures of children or grandchildren. One woman told me that the photo in her locket was of her son who lost his life in the Vietnam War. My most treasured story was a woman who had a photo in her locket that was quite old and worn. It was the only surviving picture of her mother, who perished in a concentration camp. We talked about her memories of her mother.

"I know that when I approach passengers onboard to inquire about 'what is within,' their stories will always touch me deeply and become my memories as well. I believe that people wear lockets not only to keep their cherished loved ones close to their hearts, but also because they want to share memories and stories of those who have touched their 'heart strings.'

"I chose this heart cable for my square because it reminded me of intertwined lockets and the people I've met and shared moments with along the way."

Needles Size 5mm (US 8)

Extras Cable needle (cn)
Stitch marker

Note
See *School*, p. 60 for ssk and M1.

Square
Cast on 55 sts. Work 3 ridges, inc 4 sts on last (RS) row as foll: ***Next row*** (RS) K20, M1, k1, M1, k13, M1, k1, M1, k20—59 sts. ***Beg Charts A, B, and C: Row 1*** (WS) K5, place marker (pm), then reading charts from left to right, work 3 sts Chart A, pm, 6 sts Chart B, pm, 14 sts Chart C, pm, k3, pm, 14 sts Chart C, pm, 6 sts Chart B, pm, 3 sts Chart A, pm, k5. ***2*** K3, p2, work 3 sts Chart A, 6 sts Chart B, 14 sts Chart C, p3, 14 sts Chart C, 6 sts Chart B, 3 sts Chart A, p2, k3. Cont in pats as established until 20 rows of Chart C have been worked 3 times. ***Next row*** (WS) K18, ssk, k2, k2tog, k11, ssk, k2, k2tog, k18—55 sts. K 4 rows more. Bind off. ∩

IN OTHER WORDS

1/1 RC Sl 1 to cn, hold to back, k1; k1 from cn.
1/1 LC Sl 1 to cn, hold to front, k1; k1 from cn.
1/1 RPC Sl 1 to cn, hold to back, k1; p1 from cn.
1/1 LPC Sl 1 to cn, hold to front, p1; k1 from cn.
1/2 LC Sl 1 knitwise, k2, pass sl st over 2 k sts.
2/1 RC Sl 1 to cn, hold to back, k2; k1 from cn.
2/1 LC Sl 2 to cn, hold to front, k1; k2 from cn.
2/1 RPC Sl 1 to cn, hold to back, k2; p1 from cn.
2/1 LPC Sl 2 to cn, hold to front, p1; k2 from cn.
2/2 LC Sl 2 to cn, hold to front, k2; k2 from cn.

K on RS, p on WS
P on RS, k on WS
Yo
1/1 RC on RS
1/1 RC on WS
1/1 LC on WS
1/1 RPC
1/1 LPC
1/2 LC
2/1 RC
2/1 LC
2/1 RPC
2/1 LPC
2/2 LC

CHART A *OVER 3 STS*
Row 1 (WS) P3. ***2*** 1/2 LC. ***3*** P1, yo, p1. ***4*** K3. Rep rows 1–4 for Chart A.

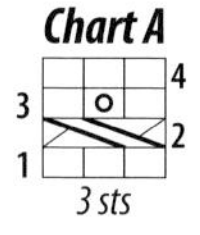

CHART B *OVER 6 STS*
Row 1 (WS) K2, p2, k2. ***2*** P2, 1/1 RC, p2. Rep rows 1 and 2 for Chart B.

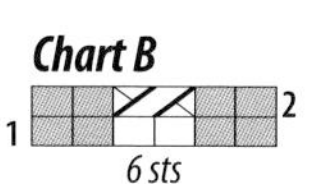

CHART C *OVER 14 STS*
Row 1 (WS) K5, p4, k5. ***2*** P5, 2/2 LC, p5. ***3 and all foll WS rows (except 19)*** K the knit sts and p the purl sts. ***4*** P4, 2/1 RPC, 2/1 LPC, p4. ***6*** P3, 2/1 RPC, p2, 2/1 LPC, p3. ***8*** P2, 2/1 RPC, p4, 2/1 LPC, p2. ***10*** P1, [2/1 RPC] twice, [2/1 LPC] twice, p1. ***12*** [2/1 RPC] twice, p2, [2/1 LPC] twice. ***14*** K1, 1/1 LPC, 2/1 LPC, p2, 2/1 RPC, 1/1 RPC, k1. ***16*** K1, p1, 1/1 LPC, 2/1 LPC, 2/1 RPC, 1/1 RPC, p1, k1. ***18*** 1/1 LPC, 1/1 RPC, p1, 2/2 LC, p1, 1/1 LPC, 1/1 RPC. ***19*** (WS) K1, 1/1 RC, k2, p4, k2, 1/1 LC, k1. ***20*** P4, 2/1 RC, 2/1 LC, p4. Rep rows 1-20 for Chart C.

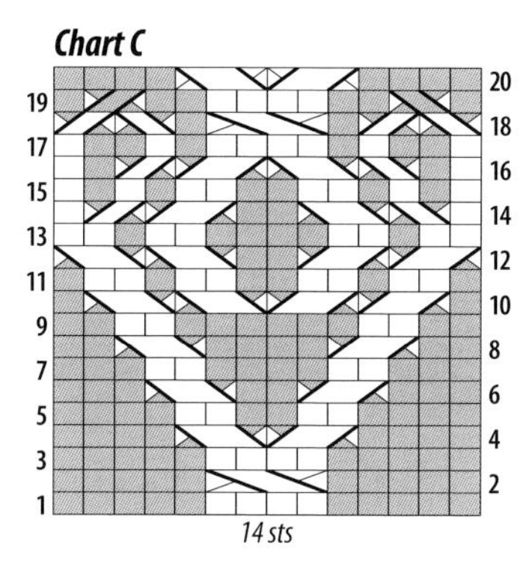

Pat Arrangement

3 sts garter st	2 sts rev St st	3 sts Chart A	6 sts Chart B	14 sts Chart C	3 sts rev St st	14 sts Chart C	6 sts Chart B	3 sts Chart A	2 sts rev St st	3 sts garter st

Jay Campbell

ELIZABETH, COLORADO

"I grew up around knitters. My first memories include watching my great-grandparents sitting on a sofa together, knitting. My mother is an avid knitter and has never been far from a project. With such great examples how could I not catch the bug sometime?

"I began knitting 15 years ago when my new bride and I decided I had way too much energy, and needed something to help me sit still while watching movies. She encouraged me to try knitting, and my needles have not been empty since. When I first read about this contest I thought it would be great to design a square. As an elementary school teacher, I am always telling my students to try new things so they can grow and learn. I took my own advice, and here is the result.

"To uphold the tradition of Aran knitting being tied to the family, I chose to represent children. Although the children depicted in my square are symbolic of children from the North, South, East, and West, I used my four as the models. Imagine the children running in four directions, and playing in the yard, with joyous laughter coming from a turn on the slide or a swing to touch the sky. I hope you enjoy knitting this square, entitled 'Play Yard,' as much as I have."

Needles Size 4mm (US 6) circular, 40cm (16") long
Five size 4mm (US 6) double-pointed needles (dpn)

Extras Cable needle (cn)

Notes

1 See *School*, p. 60 for SKP and S2KP2. **2** Work last S2KP2 over last 2 sts of rnd and fist st of next rnd.

Square

With circular needle, cast on 224 sts. Join, being careful not to twist sts, and work as foll: ***Rnd 1*** *Work rnd 1 of chart over 56 sts; rep from* 3 times more. Cont in pat through chart rnd 43, changing to dpns when necessary. Cut yarn and run tail through rem 8 sts. Pull tightly and secure.

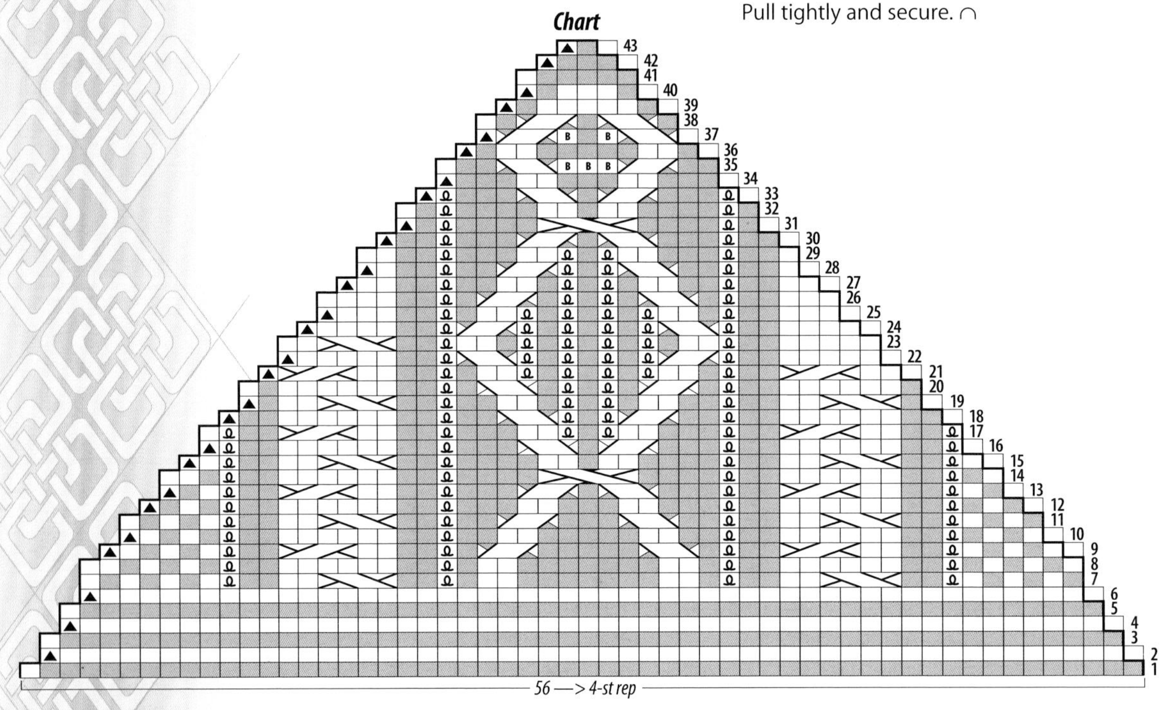

IN OTHER WORDS

MAKE BOBBLE (MB) [K1, p1] twice into a st, turn; SKP, k2tog, turn; SKP.
2/1 RC Sl 1 to cn, hold to back, k2; k1 from cn.
2/1 LC Sl 2 to cn, hold to front, k1; k2 from cn.
2/1 RPC Sl 1 to cn, hold to back, k2; p1 from cn.
2/1 LPC Sl 2 to cn, hold to front, p1; k2 from cn.
2/2 RC Sl 2 to cn, hold to back, k2; k2 from cn.
2/2 LC Sl 2 to cn, hold to front, k2; k2 from cn.
2/1/2 LPC Sl 3 to cn, hold to front, k2; sl 1 st from cn to LH needle and p it; k2 from cn.

CHART *BEG OVER 224 STS*

Rnd 1 [P55, k1] 4 times. ***2*** K1, [k53, S2KP2] 4 times. ***3*** [P53, k1] 4 times. ***4*** K1, [k51, S2KP2] 4 times. ***5*** [P51, k1] 4 times. ***6*** K1, [k49, S2KP2] 4 times. ***7*** [(P1, k1) 3 times, *k1 through back loop (tbl), p2, 2/2 LC, k2, p2, k1 tbl*, p1, k2, p7, k2, p1, work from * to * once, (k1, p1) 3 times, k1] 4 times. ***8*** [(K1, p1) 3 times, *k1 tbl, p2, k6, p2, k1 tbl*, p1, k2, p7, k2, p1, work from * to * once, (p1, k1) 3 times, k1] 4 times. ***9*** K1, [(k1, p1) twice, k1, *k1 tbl, p2, k2, 2/2 RC, p2, k1 tbl*, p1, 2/1 LPC, p5, 2/1 RPC, p1, work from * to * once, (k1, p1) twice, k1, S2KP2] 4 times. ***10*** K1, [(k1, p1) twice, *k1 tbl, p2, k6, p2, k1 tbl*, p2, k2, p5, k2, p2, work from * to * once, (p1, k1) twice, S2KP2] 4 times. ***11*** [(P1, k1) twice, *k1 tbl, p2, 2/2 LC, k2, p2, k1 tbl*, p2, 2/1 LPC, p3, 2/1 RPC, p2, work from * to * once, (k1, p1) twice, k1] 4 times. ***12*** K1, [p1, k1, p1, *k1 tbl, p2, k6, p2, k1 tbl*, (p3, k2) twice, p3, work from * to * once, p1, k1, p1, S2KP2] 4 times. ***13*** K1, [p1, k1, *k1 tbl, p2, k2, 2/2 RC, p2, k1 tbl*, p3, 2/1 LPC, p1, 2/1 RPC, p3, work from * to * once, k1, p1, S2KP2] 4 times. ***14*** [K1, p1, *k1 tbl, p2, k6, p2, k1 tbl*, p4, 2/1/2 LPC, p4, work from * to * once, p1, k2] 4 times. ***15*** K1, [k1, *k1 tbl, p2, 2/2 LC, k2, p2, k1 tbl*, p4, k2, p1, k2, p4, work from * to * once, k1, S2KP2] 4 times. ***16*** K1, [*k1 tbl, p2, k6, p2, k1 tbl*, p3, 2/1 RC, p1, 2/1 LC, p3, work from * to * once, S2KP2] 4 times. ***17*** [*K1 tbl, p2, k2, 2/2 RC, p2, k1 tbl*, p3, k2, k1 tbl, p1, k1 tbl, k2, p3, work from * to * once, k1] 4 times. ***18*** K1, [p2, k6, p2, k1 tbl, p2, 2/1 RPC, k1 tbl, p1, k1 tbl, 2/1 LPC, p2, k1 tbl, p2, k6, p2, S2KP2] 4 times. ***19*** K1, [p1, 2/2 LC, k2, p2, k1 tbl, p2, k2, (p1, k1 tbl) twice, p1, k2, p2, k1 tbl, p2, 2/2 LC, k2, p1, S2KP2] 4 times. ***20*** [P1, k6, p2, k1 tbl, p1, 2/1 RC, (p1, k1 tbl) twice, p1, 2/1 LC, p1, k1 tbl, p2, k6, p1, k1] 4 times. ***21*** K1, [k2, 2/2 RC, p2, k1 tbl, p1, k2, (k1 tbl, p1) 3 times, k1 tbl, k2, p1, k1 tbl, p2, k2, 2/2 RC, S2KP2] 4 times. ***22*** K1, [k5, p2, k1 tbl, 2/1 RPC, (k1 tbl, p1) 3 times, k1 tbl, 2/1 LPC, k1 tbl, p2, k5, S2KP2] 4 times. ***23*** [K5, p2, k1 tbl, k2, (p1, k1 tbl) 4 times, p1, k2, k1 tbl, p2, 2/2 LC, k2] 4 times. ***24*** K1, [k4, p2, k1 tbl, 2/1 LPC, (k1 tbl, p1) 3 times, k1 tbl, 2/1 RPC, k1 tbl, p2, k4, S2KP2] 4 times. ***25*** K1, [k3, p2, k1 tbl, p1, k2, (k1 tbl, p1) 3 times, k1 tbl, k2, p1, k1 tbl, p2, k3, S2KP2] 4 times. ***26*** [K3, p2, k1 tbl, p1, 2/1 LPC, (p1, k1 tbl) twice, p1, 2/1 RPC, p1, k1 tbl, p2, k4] 4 times. ***27*** K1, [k2, p2, k1 tbl, p2, k2, (p1, k1 tbl) twice, p1, k2, p2, k1 tbl, p2, k2, S2KP2] 4 times. ***28*** K1, [k1, p2, k1 tbl, p2, 2/1 LPC, k1 tbl, p1, k1 tbl, 2/1 RPC, p2, k1 tbl, p2, k1, S2KP2] 4 times. ***29*** [K1, p2, k1 tbl, p3, k2, k1 tbl, p1, k1 tbl, k2, p3, k1 tbl, p2, k2] 4 times. ***30*** K1, [p2, k1 tbl, p3, 2/1 LPC, p1, 2/1 RPC, p3, k1 tbl, p2, S2KP2] 4 times. ***31*** K1, [p1, k1 tbl, p4, 2/1/2 LPC, p4, k1 tbl, p1, S2KP2] 4 times. ***32*** [P1, k1 tbl, p4, k2, p1, k2, p4, k1 tbl, p1, k1] 4 times. ***33*** K1, [k1 tbl, p3, 2/1 RPC, p1, 2/1 LPC, p3, k1 tbl, S2KP2] 4 times. ***34*** K1, [(p3, k2) twice, p3, S2KP2] 4 times. ***35*** [P2, 2/1 RPC, (MB) 3 times, 2/1 LPC, p2, k1] 4 times. ***36*** K1, [p1, k2, p5, k2, p1, S2KP2] 4 times. ***37*** K1, [2/1 LPC, MB, p1, MB, 2/1 RPC, S2KP2] 4 times. ***38*** [P1, 2/1 LPC, p1, 2/1 RPC, p1, k1] 4 times. ***39*** K1, [p1, k5, p1, S2KP2] 4 times. ***40*** K1, [p1, k3, p1, S2KP2] 4 times. ***41*** [P5, k1] 4 times. ***42*** K1, [p3, S2KP2] 4 times. ***43*** K1, [p1, S2KP2] 4 times.

- Knit
- Purl
- K1 through back loop (tbl)
- Make Bobble (MB)
- S2KP2
- 2/1 RC
- 2/1 LC
- 2/1 RPC
- 2/1 LPC
- 2/2 RC
- 2/2 LC
- 2/1/2 LPC

Dana Hurt

JONESBORO, ARKANSAS

"Like so many knitters, I was exposed to knitting by my grandmother when I was a child. Although I knitted infrequently during my teens, I took up the hobby seriously by the age of twenty-five. During my career as a flight attendant I met two other 'serious' knitters who have become dear friends and a great source of inspiration and motivation.

"My interests—art, graphic design, antiques, and genealogy—along with input from my two knitting friends are the sources from which I drew the design idea for my Aran block. I put together a combination that balances the heavier center cable with a lacy cable and small twisted-rib cables for weight. This design would also be appropriate for a paneled afghan, or the pattern can be repeated to the desired width and knit to any length. The back also has a pleasing look, a bonus you don't always get with patterns."

Needles Size 4.5mm (US 7)

Extras Cable needle (cn)

Square
Cast on 54 sts. Work 3 ridges, working last row as foll: **Next row** (WS) K19, k into front and back of next st (inc 1), [k2, inc 1] 5 times, k19—60 sts. ***Beg Chart pats: Row 1*** (RS) K3, work Chart A over 7 sts, work 4 sts Chart B, 4 sts Chart A, 24 sts Chart C, 4 sts Chart D, 4 sts Chart E, work Chart D over 7 sts, k3. ***2*** K3, then reading charts from left to right, work 7 sts Chart D, 4 sts Chart E, 4 sts Chart D, 24 sts Chart C, 4 sts Chart A, 4 sts Chart B, 7 sts Chart A, k3. Cont in pats as established until 16 rows of Chart C have been worked 4 times, then work rows 1-15 once more. ***Next row*** (WS) K19, [k2tog, k2] 5 times, k2tog, k19—54 sts. Work 3 ridges. Bind off. ∩

YO BEFORE A K ST

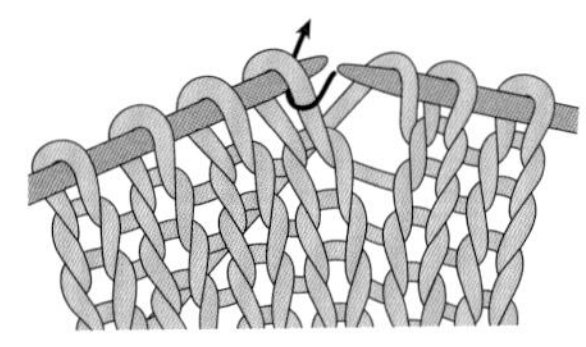

Bring yarn to front, then to back over needle, k next st.

YO BEFORE A P ST

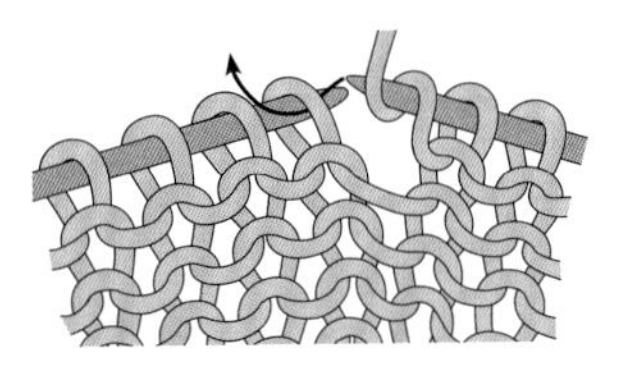

With yarn in front of needle, bring yarn over needle and to front again, p next st.

IN OTHER WORDS

1/1 RC Sl 1 to cn, hold to back, k1; k1 from cn.
1/1 LC Sl 1 to cn, hold to front, k1; k1 from cn.
2/1 RPC Sl 1 to cn, hold to back, k2; p1 from cn.
2/1 LPC Sl 2 to cn, hold to front, p1; k2 from cn.
2/2 RC Sl 2 to cn, hold to back, k2; k2 from cn.
2/2 LC Sl 2 to cn, hold to front, k2; k2 from cn.
2/2 RPC Sl 2 to cn, hold to back, k2; p2 from cn.
2/2 LPC Sl 2 to cn, hold to front, p2; k2 from cn.

CHART A *MULTIPLE OF 3 STS, PLUS 1*
Row 1 (RS) *P1, 1/1 RC; rep from*, p1. ***2*** K1, *p2, k1; rep from*. Rep rows 1 and 2 for Chart A.

CHART B *OVER 4 STS*
Rows 1, 3, 5, 9, 11, 13 and 15 K2, yo, k2tog. ***2 and all WS rows*** P2, yo, p2tog. ***7*** 2/2 LC. ***16*** Rep row 2. Rep rows 1–16 for Chart B.

CHART C *OVER 24 STS*
Row 1 (RS) P2, 2/2 RC, [p4, 2/2 RC] twice, p2. ***2 and all WS rows*** K the knit sts and p the purl sts. ***3*** P1, 2/1 RPC, [2/2 LPC, 2/2 RPC] twice, 2/1 LPC, p1. ***5*** 2/1 RPC, p3, 2/2 LC, p4, 2/2 LC, p3, 2/1 LPC. ***7*** K2, p2, [2/2 RPC, 2/2 LPC] twice, p2, k2. ***9*** K2, p2, k2, p4, 2/2 RC, p4, k2, p2, k2. ***11*** K2, p2, [2/2 LPC, 2/2 RPC] twice, p2, k2. ***13*** 2/1 LPC, p3, 2/2 LC, p4, 2/2 LC, p3, 2/1 RPC. ***15*** P1, 2/1 LPC, [2/2 RPC, 2/2 LPC] twice, 2/1 RPC, p1. ***16*** Rep row 2. Rep rows 1–16 for Chart C.

CHART D *MULTIPLE OF 3 STS, PLUS 1*
Row 1 (RS) *P1, 1/1 LC; rep from*, p1. ***2*** K1, *p2, k1; rep from*. Rep rows 1 and 2 for Chart D.

CHART E *OVER 4 STS*
Rows 1, 3, 5, 9, 11, 13 and 15 K2tog, yo, k2. ***2 and all WS rows*** P2tog, yo, p2. ***7*** 2/2 RC. ***16*** Rep row 2. Rep rows 1–16 for Chart E.

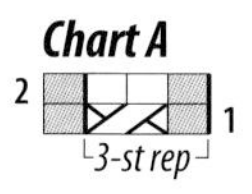

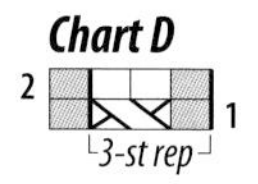

Chart B
4 sts

Chart E
4 sts

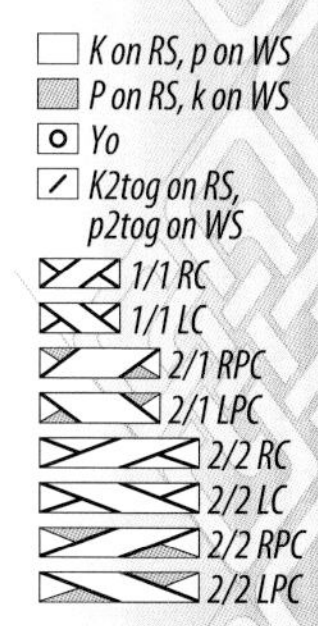

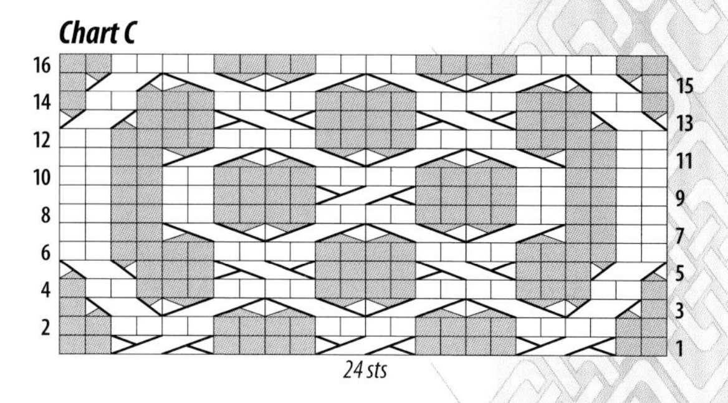

Pat Arrangement

3 sts garter st	7 sts Chart D	4 sts Chart E	4 sts Chart D	24 sts Chart C	4 sts Chart A	4 sts Chart B	7 sts Chart A	3 sts garter st

Carol Adams

MISSISSAUGA, ONTARIO, CANADA

"Eleven years ago, a work promotion required commuting by train. It was easy to pick up the needles and knit with a group of 'needlewomen' who rode the same train each morning. However, after 31 years as a Court Administrator and Justice of the Peace, I retired in 1997. My mother, now 86, has also picked up her needles again, and we spend happy spring and summer months sitting together and knitting on the deck of our cottage.

"I am recognized by The Knitting Guild of Canada as a Master Knitter and am an active member of the West Toronto Knitters' Guild.

"The inspiration for this design came from the incomparable Lily Chin's Reversible Cables class. The challenge involved knitting the gauge-required number of stitches to simultaneously produce traditional Aran components on each face without the bulk of a second layer."

Needles Size 4mm (US 6)

Extras Cable needle (cn)

Note

See *School*, p. 60 for ssk and Make 1 knit (M1K) and Make 1 purl (M1P).

Square

Cast on 55 sts. Work 3 ridges, end with a WS row. ***Beg Chart pats: Row 1*** (RS) K3, work 6 sts Chart A, Chart B over 4 sts (inc'd to 8), 6 sts Chart A, 17 sts Chart C, 6 sts Chart A, Chart D over 4 sts (inc'd to 8), 6 sts Chart A, k3—63 sts. Keeping first and last 3 sts in garter st (k every row), work charts as established over center 57 sts until 73 total chart rows have been worked (ending with row 1 of Charts A and C, and row 7 of Charts B and D). ***Next row*** (WS) K3, work 6 sts Chart A, [p2tog, ssk] twice, 6 sts Chart A, k17, 6 sts Chart A, [ssk, p2tog] twice, 6 sts Chart A, k3—55 sts. Work 3 ridges. Bind off. ∩

Pat Arrangement

3 sts garter st	6 sts Chart A	4 to 8 sts Chart D	6 sts Chart A	17 sts Chart C	6 sts Chart A	4 to 8 sts Chart B	6 sts Chart A	3 sts garter st

IN OTHER WORDS

4/4 KPLC Sl 4 to cn, hold to front, k2, p2; [k2, p2] from cn.
4/4 PKRC Sl 4 to cn, hold to back, p2, k2; [p2, k2] from cn.

CHART A *OVER 6 STS*

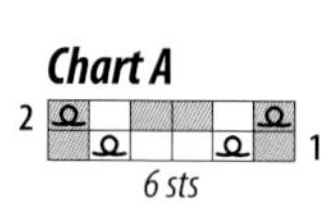

Row 1 (RS) P1, k1 through back loop (tbl), k2, k1 tbl, p1. ***2*** K1 tbl, p1, k2, p1, k1 tbl.
Rep rows 1 and 2 for Chart A.

CHART B *OVER 4 STS, INC'D TO 8 STS*

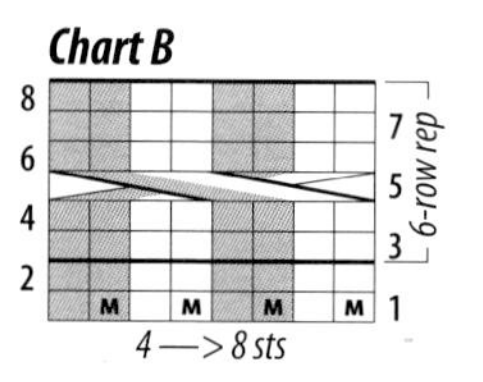

Row 1 (RS) [M1K, k1, M1P, p1] twice—8 sts. ***2, 3, 4, 6, 7, 8*** [K2, p2] twice. ***5*** 4/4 KPLC. Rep rows 3–8 for Chart B.

CHART C *OVER 17 STS*

Row 1 (RS) K6, k2tog, yo, k1, yo, ssk, k6. ***2 and all WS rows*** Knit. ***3*** K5, k2tog, yo, k3, yo, ssk, k5. ***5*** K4, k2tog, yo, k5, yo, ssk, k4. ***7*** K3, k2tog, yo, k7, yo, ssk, k3. ***9*** K2, k2tog, yo, k9, yo, ssk, k2. ***11*** K1, k2tog, yo, k11, yo, ssk, k1. ***13*** K1, yo, ssk, k11, k2tog, yo, k1. ***15*** K2, yo, ssk, k9, k2tog, yo, k2. ***17*** K3, yo, ssk, k7, k2tog, yo, k3. ***19*** K4, yo, ssk, k5, k2tog, yo, k4. ***21*** K5, yo, ssk, k3, k2tog, yo, k5. ***23*** K6, yo, ssk, k1, k2tog, yo, k6. ***24*** Knit.
Rep rows 1–24 for Chart C.

CHART D *OVER 4 STS, INC'D TO 8 STS*

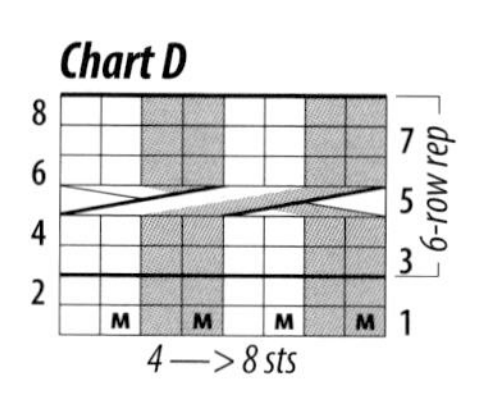

Row 1 (RS) [M1P, p1, M1K, k1] twice—8 sts. ***2, 3, 4, 6, 7, 8*** [P2, k2] twice. ***5*** 4/4 PKRC. Rep rows 3–8 for Chart D.

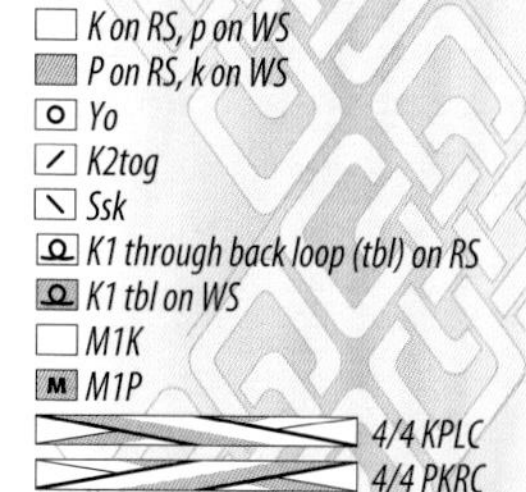

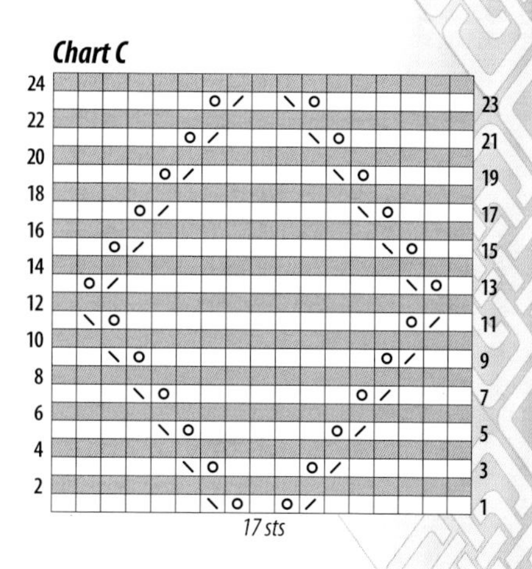

Betty Salpekar

JONESTOWN, NORTH CAROLINA

"I have been knitting steadily and happily for over thirty years, though my hobby has only approached the status of a compulsion in the last ten years or so. I've done a lot of knitting in 1/12th scale (1 inch = 1 foot) using needles I made from piano wire, but as my vision ages I find myself sticking mostly to full-size knitting. I am more of an architect in my knitting than a decorator. I find deep satisfaction in 'building' a knitted item in new ways, or at least in ways that are new to me.

"In my square, I wanted an unusual cable design for the center, so I charted part of the Celtic knot that appears as a cover decoration on Alice Starmore's The Celtic Collection. *I enjoyed devising ways to make those three interwoven 'cords' appear smoothly closed. I wanted the frame for the center square to be composed of continuous, interwoven closed cords, too, and a classic Aran three-strand braid worked well."*

Needles Size 3.75mm (US 5)
Two size 3.75mm (US 5) double-pointed needles (dpn)
Size 5 circular, 40cm (24") long

Extras Cable needle (cn)
Stitch markers
Size 4.00mm (F/5) crochet hook

Pat Arrangement

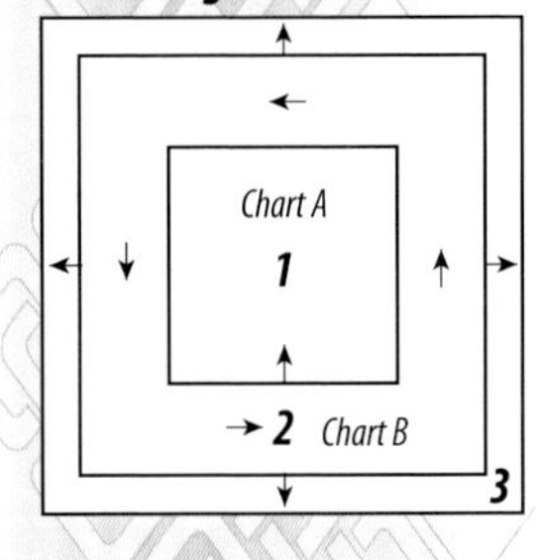

Chain st seam

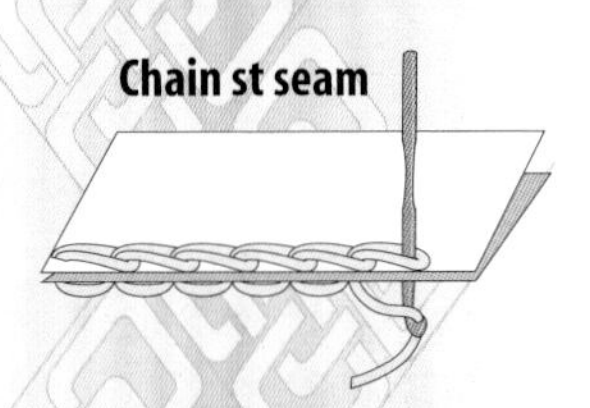

Notes

1 See *School*, p. 60 for ssk, ssp, invisible cast-on and grafting. **2** Work center square (1) first, then cable border (2), then garter border (3). **3** Sl sts purlwise with yarn at WS, unless otherwise indicated.

Center Square (1)

Cast on 38 sts. Work 55 rows of Chart A. Bind off.

Cable Border (2)

Wrap st and Turn (W&T) With yarn in back, sl 1, bring yarn to front, sl st back to LH needle, move yarn to back (1 st wrapped), turn work.

Hide Wrap for a Knit st (HKW) K wrap and st tog.

Hide Wrap for a Purl st (HPW) Insert RH needle from front to back under wrap and lift wrap over and behind st on LH needle; p st and wrap tog.

Invisibly cast on 15 sts. *Work 8 rows of Chart B 6 times, then work rows 1–7 once more. ***Work mitred corner: Row 1*** (RS) P1, k1, p2, k2, p2, 2/2 RC, p2, W&T. ***WS rows 2-14*** Sl 1, then k the knit sts and p the purl sts across. ***3*** P1, k1, p2, 2/1 LPC, 2/1 RPC, sl 2 to cn, hold to front, p1, sl 2 from cn to LH needle, k1, W&T. ***5*** P1, k1, p3, 2/2 LC, p1, W&T. ***7*** P1, k1, p2, 2/1 RPC, sl 2 to cn, hold to front, p1, sl 2 from cn to LH needle, W&T. ***9*** P1, k1, p2, k2, W&T. ***11*** P1, k1, p2, W&T. ***13*** P1, k1, W&T. ***15*** P1, sl 1, turn. ***16*** P1 (yarn comes from 1 st to the left), k1. ***17*** P1, k1, HPW, sl 1, turn. ***18*** K2, p1, k1. ***19*** P1, k1, p2, HKW, sl 1, turn. ***20*** P2, k2, p1, k1. ***21*** P1, k1, p2, k2, HPW, sl 1, turn. ***22*** K2, p2, k2, p1, k1. ***23*** P1, k1, p2, 2/1 LPC, sl 1 to cn, hold to back, HKW, k1; return st on cn to RH needle, turn. ***24*** With RH needle, lift any strand that is between needles (and slightly towards WS) up to LH needle and k it tog with first st on needle (this closes a hole that would otherwise form), p4, k3, p1, k1. ***25*** P1, k1, p3, 2/2 LC, p1, HPW, sl 1, turn. ***26*** P1, k2, p4, k3, p1, k1. ***27*** P1, k1, p2, 2/1 RPC, 2/1 LPC, sl 1 to cn, hold to back, k1, HKW, p1 from cn, turn. ***28*** Lift a strand up to LH needle as for row 24, sl 1 st from RH to LH needle and k st and strand tog, k1, p4, k2, p2, k2, p1, k1. ***29*** P1, k1, p2, k2, p2, 2/2 RC, p2, HPW.

Rep from* 3 times more, ending last rep with row 28. ***Next row*** (RS) Sl 8 sts to RH needle, then sl 2 to cn and hold to back, sl 2 to RH needle, sl 2 from cn to LH needle, then return all sts on RH needle to LH needle (this puts sts in proper order for grafting). Place cast-on sts on dpn and graft open sts to cast-on sts (see illustration, p. 55).

Finishing

Sew cable border to center square. With crochet hook, work chain st over seam by pulling up loops from yarn held at WS (see illustration, left). With ends of yarn, sew cable sections from chart rows 4 and 52 securely to square. Close up any holes with other yarn ends.

Garter st Border (3)

With RS facing and circular needle, beg at a corner and *pick up and k56 sts along side edge, place marker, pick up and k1 st at corner; rep from* 3 times more—228 sts. Join

and work as foll: ***Rnd 1*** [P into front and back of next st, p to 1 st before marker, p into front and back of next st, slip marker, p1] 4 times—236 sts. **2** Knit. Rep last 2 rnds once more—244 sts. Turn work and bind off knitwise.

Special Instructions (SI)

A With separate yarn and dpn, invisibly cast on 3 sts. [P 1 row, k 1 row] twice. Cut yarn. Place cast-on sts (removing waste yarn), on another dpn. Place 3 sts of either dpn (with knit side facing) on LH needle, then with RH needle, k2tog, ssk, p2, sl 1, place 3 sts from 2nd dpn on LH needle (twisting needle so the knit side is facing), sl 1 from RH needle to LH needle, k2tog, ssk.

B Work as for SI-A, except work 6 rows in St st instead of 4 and p4 instead of p2 between ssk and sl 1.

C Insert LH needle from front to back under 2nd strand down between st just worked and first st on LH needle and work into strand as foll: k into back and front of st, yo, k into front—4 sts; turn, p1, sl 2, p1, turn; k4.

D P next 2 sts onto a dpn and hold to RS of work, then with RH needle, k into front and back of next 2 sts on LH needle, p next 2 sts onto a 2nd dpn. Bring dpn to RS of work and using a separate 10" strand of yarn, graft sts on dpns tog using St st graft.

E Work as for SI-A, with these changes: Work 2 rows St st, instead of 4. When placing sts on LH needle, place them with purl side facing and make sure that 3-st cord falls to RS of work. Then with RH needle, ssp, p2tog, k2, place 3 sts from 2nd dpn on LH needle (making sure cord is not twisted), ssp, p2tog.

F P into front and back of next st, [sl next 2 sts to a dpn] twice. With a separate strand, graft sts on dpns tog, then p into front and back of next st on LH needle. (After square is finished, run tail from grafting through back of p sts to close hole.)

G Sl next 2 sts to dpn and leave in front of work, p into front and back of next 2 sts. With a separate strand, [p 1 row, k1 row, p 1 row] over 2 sts on dpn. Sl next 2 sts from LH needle to a 2nd dpn. Graft sts on dpns tog.

H Sl next 2 sts to dpn and leave in front of work, [p into front and back of next st, p1] twice. With a separate strand, [k 1 row, p1 row] twice over 2 sts on dpn. Complete as for SI-G.

(In Other Words continues on p. 55 along with grafting illustration)

2/1 RPC (on RS) Sl 1 to cn, hold to back, k2; p1 from cn.
(on WS) Sl 2 to cn, hold to back, k1; p2 from cn.

2/1 LPC (on RS) Sl 2 to cn, hold to front, p1; k2 from cn.
(on WS) Sl 1 to cn, hold to front, p2; k1 from cn.

2/2 RC Sl 2 to cn, hold to back, k2; k2 from cn.

2/2 LC Sl 2 to cn, hold to front, k2; k2 from cn.

2/2 RPC (on RS or WS) Sl 2 to cn, hold to back, k2; p2 from cn.

2/2 LPC (on RS or WS) Sl 2 to cn, hold to front, p2; k2 from cn.

K on RS, p on WS
P on RS, k on WS
Ssp
P2tog
No sts exist in these areas of chart
2/1 RPC
2/1 LPC
2/2 RC
2/2 LC
2/2 RPC
2/2 LPC
A B C D E F G H See Special Instructions

Chart B

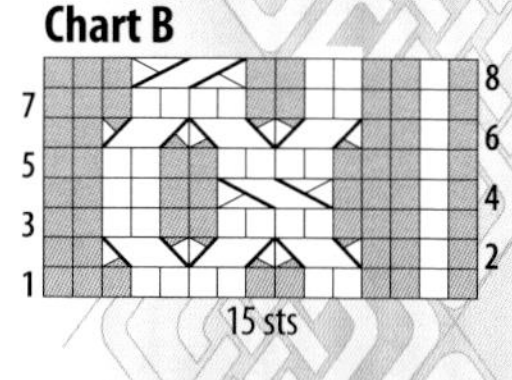

Chart A

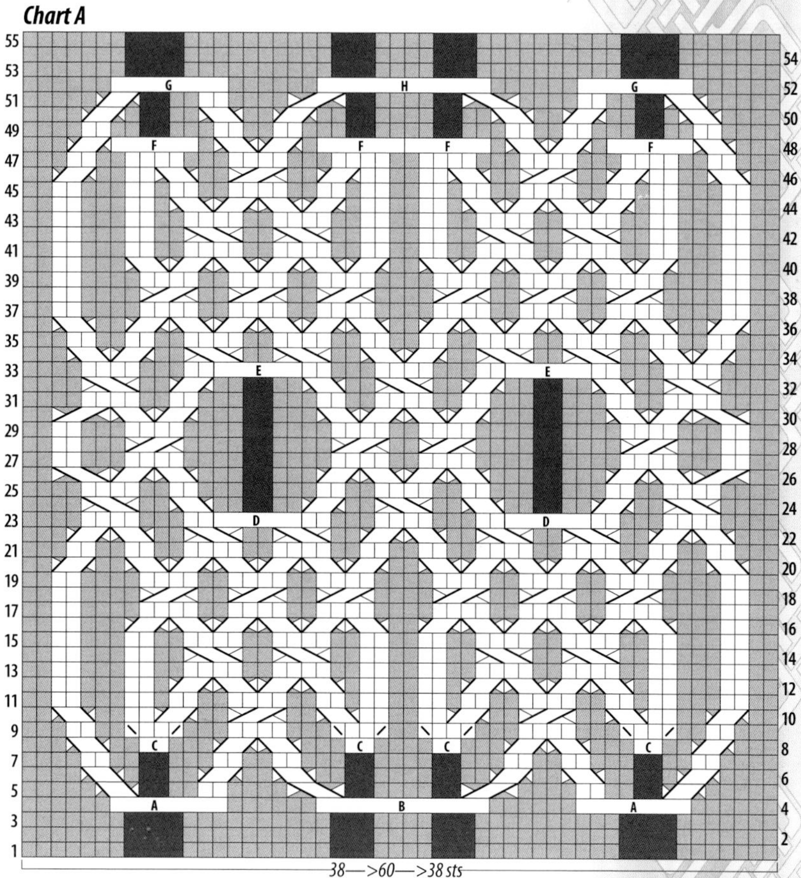

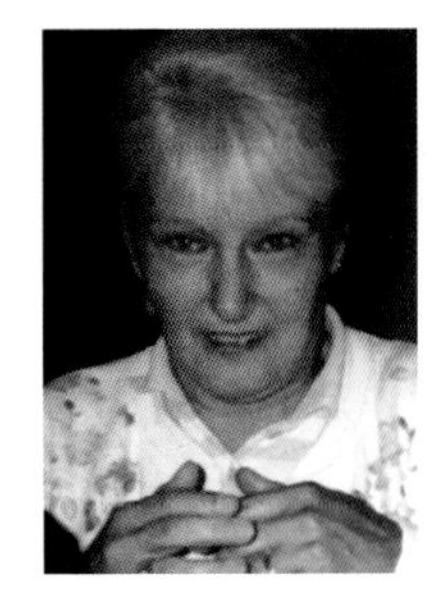

Georgia Vincent

PITTSFIELD, NEW HAMPSHIRE

"I have been knitting since age six. I didn't get into designing until eight years ago. I most enjoy using stitches to create pictures or designs. I try to recreate Old World architecture. Finding and using stitch combinations that define the beautiful, detailed craftsmanship in old buildings and fireplaces is a great challenge. This square uses these elements."

Needles Size 5mm (US 8) circular, 40cm (16") long
Four size 5mm (US 8) double-pointed needles (dpn)
Cable needle (cn)

Notes

1 See *School*, p. 60, for S2KP2. ***2*** Work last S2KP2 over last 2 sts of rnd and first st of next rnd.

Square

With circular needle, cast on 212 sts. Join, being careful not to twist sts. ***Rnd 1*** Work 53-st rep of chart 4 times. Work through chart rnd 37, changing to dpns when necessary—8 sts. Cut yarn, leaving a 30" tail for working center bobble. Run tail through sts, pull tightly and secure, but do not cut yarn. Pull a loop up at center then draw tail of yarn to RS next to loop, and work MB using loop as st. Fasten off.

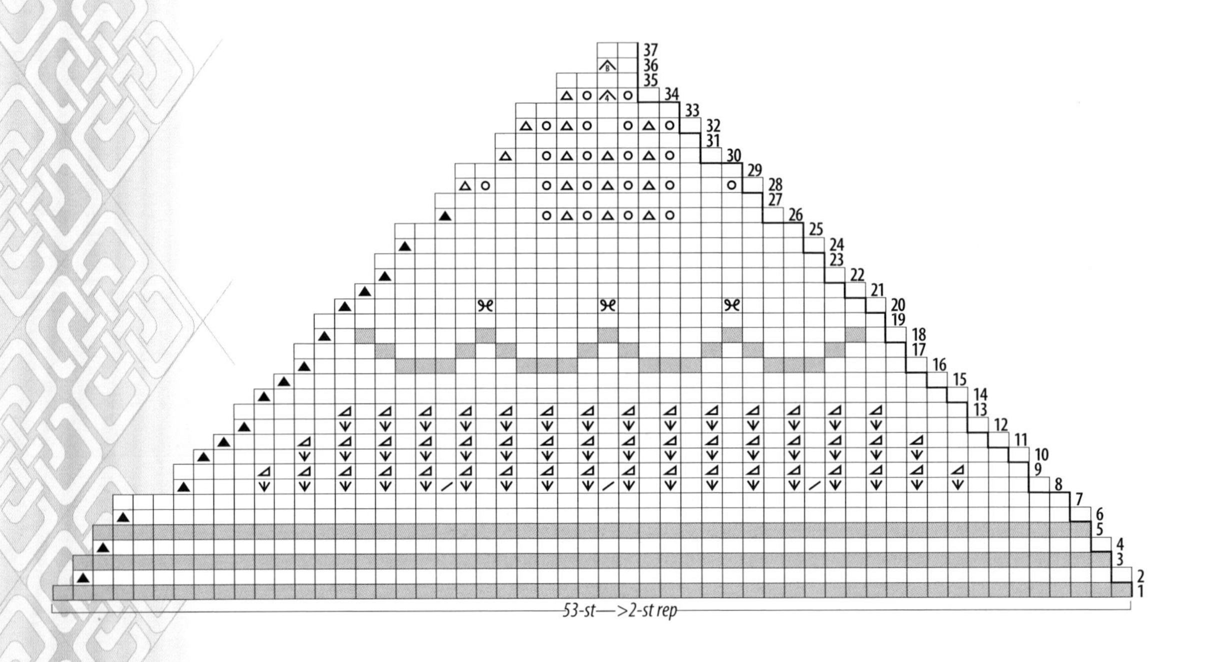

IN OTHER WORDS

INC 2 Yo, k1, yo.

DEC 2 Sl 1 knitwise, k1, psso, sl st from RH needle to LH needle, pass 2nd st on LH needle over first, sl st to RH needle.

DEC 4 Sl 1 knitwise, k2tog, psso, k2tog, sl 2 sts from RH needle to LH needle, pass 2nd st on LH needle over first, sl st to RH needle.

MAKE BOBBLE (MB) [(K1, p1) twice, k1] in st, turn, [(k1, p1) twice, k1, turn] 3 times, sl 2 tog knitwise, k3tog, pass 2 sl sts tog over k3tog.

DEC MB Work Dec 2 except do not sl st back to RH needle at end, then work MB.

Knit
Purl
Yo
S2KP2
Inc 2
K2tog
K3tog
Sl 1 to cn and wrap yarn 4x counterclockwise around this stitch. Sl st to RH needle.
Dec 2
Dec 4
Dec MB

CHART *BEG ON 212 STS*

Rnds 1, 3 and 5 Purl. ***2*** K1, [k50, S2KP2] 4 times. ***4*** K1, [k48, S2KP2] 4 times. ***6*** K1, [k46, S2KP2] 4 times. ***7*** Knit. ***8*** K1, [k3, (Inc 2, k1) 3 times, Inc 2, k2tog, (Inc 2, k1) 4 times, Inc 2, k2tog, (Inc 2, k1) 3 times, Inc 2, k2tog, (Inc 2, k1) 4 times, Inc 2, k3, S2KP2] 4 times. ***9*** [K3, (k3tog, k1) 18 times, k3] 4 times. ***10*** K1, [k4, (Inc 2, k1) 16 times, k3, S2KP2] 4 times. ***11*** K1, [k3, (k3tog, k1) 16 times, k2, S2KP2] 4 times. ***12*** K1, [k4, (Inc 2, k1) 14 times, k3, S2KP2] 4 times. ***13*** [K4, (k3tog, k1) 14 times, k4] 4 times. ***14*** K1, [k33, S2KP2] 4 times. ***15*** K1, [k31, S2KP2] 4 times. ***16*** K1, [k4, (p3, k3) 4 times, k1, S2KP2] 4 times. ***17*** [K3, p1, (k3, p1, k1, p1) 3 times, k3, p1, k4] 4 times. ***18*** K1, [k1, p1, (k5, p1) 4 times, k1, S2KP2] 4 times. ***19*** Knit. ***20*** K1, [k6, (sl 1 to cn. Wrap yarn 4x counter-clockwise around this st. Sl st to right needle, k5) 3 times, k1, S2KP2] 4 times. ***21*** [K to last 2 sts in repeat, S2KP2] 4 times. ***22*** K1, [k21, S2KP2] 4 times. ***23 and all foll odd-numbered rnds*** Knit. ***24*** K1, [k19, S2KP2] 4 times. ***26*** K1, [k4, (yo, Dec 2) 3 times, yo, k4, S2KP2] 4 times. ***28*** K1, [yo, k2, (yo, Dec 2) 3 times, yo, k2, yo, Dec 2] 4 times. ***30*** K1, [k1, (yo, Dec 2) 3 times, yo, k1, Dec 2] 4 times. ***32*** K1, [yo, Dec 2, yo, k1, (yo, Dec 2) twice] 4 times. ***34*** K1, [yo, Dec 4, yo, Dec 2] 4 times. ***36*** [K1, Dec MB] 4 times. ***37*** Knit.

Suzanne Atkinson

ORLEANS, ONTARIO, CANADA

"I have been knitting since the early '80s, when I took up knitting as a relief from my nursing studies in college. Knitting offers creativity, stability, and calm in a busy household with four children and a supportive husband.

"I am a Knitting Guild of Canada Master Knitter. As a result of participating in the program in 1994, I developed an interest in design, contests, and teaching. My square was inspired by a little country church not far from our home. It reflects the importance of my Christian faith. Like knitting in the midst of chaos, the church rests in a pastoral setting on the Ottawa River not far from the busy nation's capital.

"The simple lines of the design remind me of a child's drawing, much like those on our kitchen walls. (I resisted the urge to stitch a smiley face on the sun.) I also noticed the uncanny similarity between my square and the Schoolhouse Press logo. I like to think of this as "divine knitting synchronicity"! My square is a tribute to Meg Swansen and Elizabeth Zimmermann, who have both inspired me."

Needles Size 4mm (US 6)
Two size 4mm (US 6) double-pointed needles (dpn)

Extras Cable needle (cn)

K on RS, p on WS
P on RS, k on WS
K1 through back loop (tbl)
M1 knit (M1K)
M1 purl (M1P)
P2tog
Ssk
K2tog
Make Bobble (MB)
Make Small Bobble (MSB)
Sl 1 purlwise with yarn at WS
Sts do not exist in these areas of chart
1/1 RPC
1/1 LPC
2/1 RPC
2/1 LPC
1/2 RPC
1/2 LPC
2/2 RC
2/2 LC
2/2 RPC
2/2 LPC
2/2 PKLC
Inc 2
Dec 4

Notes

1 See *School*, p. 60, for ssk, Make 1 knit (M1K) and Make 1 purl (M1P). **2** Sun's rays are worked separately and attached.

Square

Cast on 65 sts. Work 3 ridges, end with a WS row. ***Next row*** (RS) K3, *p1, k1 through back loop (tbl); rep from* to last 4 sts, p1, k3. ***Next row*** Knit. Rep last 2 rows 4 times more. Keeping first and last 3 sts in garter st (k every row), work pat over center 59 sts as foll: Work rows 1–67 of Chart Pat, then work 5 rows in rev St st (p on RS, k on WS). Work 3 ridges over all sts. Bind off.

Finishing

Sun's rays *MAKE 6*

With dpns, cast on 3 sts. Work I-cord for 1". Cut yarn, leaving a 5" tail. Run tail through open sts and pull tog tightly. Weave cast-on tail through length of cord. Use 5" tail to sew cords in place in relation to sun, using photo as guide.

IN OTHER WORDS

MAKE BOBBLE (MB) ***Note:*** Do not turn at end of rows; sl sts back to LH needle at end of rows 1-3. ***1*** [(K1, yo) twice, k1] in st. ***2*** K5. ***3*** Ssk, k1, k2tog. ***4*** K3, then pass 2nd and 3rd sts, one at a time, over first st.

MAKE SMALL BOBBLE (MSB) [K1, p1] 3 times in st, pass 2nd, 3rd, 4th, 5th and 6th sts, one at a time, over first st.

INC 2 K into back, then front of st, then insert LH needle behind the vertical strand that runs between 2 sts just made and k strand tbl (see ill).

DEC 4 Sl 3 with yarn in front, *pass 2nd st on RH needle over first (center) st, sl center st back to LH needle and pass 2nd st on LH needle over it*, sl center st to RH needle, rep from *to* once more, k center st.

1/1 RPC Sl 1 to cn, hold to back, k1; p1 from cn.
1/1 LPC Sl 1 to cn, hold to front, p1; k1 from cn.
2/1 RPC Sl 1 to cn, hold to back, k2; p1 from cn.
2/1 LPC Sl 2 to cn, hold to front, p1; k2 from cn.
1/2 RPC Sl 2 to cn, hold to back, k1; p2 from cn.
1/2 LPC Sl 1 to cn, hold to front, p2; k1 from cn.
2/2 RC Sl 2 to cn, hold to back, k2; k2 from cn.
2/2 LC Sl 2 to cn, hold to front, k2; k2 from cn.
2/2 RPC Sl 2 to cn, hold to back, k2; p2 from cn.
2/2 LPC Sl 2 to cn, hold to front, p2; k2 from cn.
2/2 PKLC Sl 2 to cn, hold to front, p1, k1; [k1, p1] from cn.

(continues on p. 57)

INC 2

UNATTACHED I-CORD

I-cord is a tiny tube of stockinette stitch, made with 2 double-pointed needles.

1 Cast on 3 or 4 sts.

2 Knit. Do not turn work. Slide stitches to opposite end of needle. Repeat Step 2 until cord is the desired length.

Chart Pat

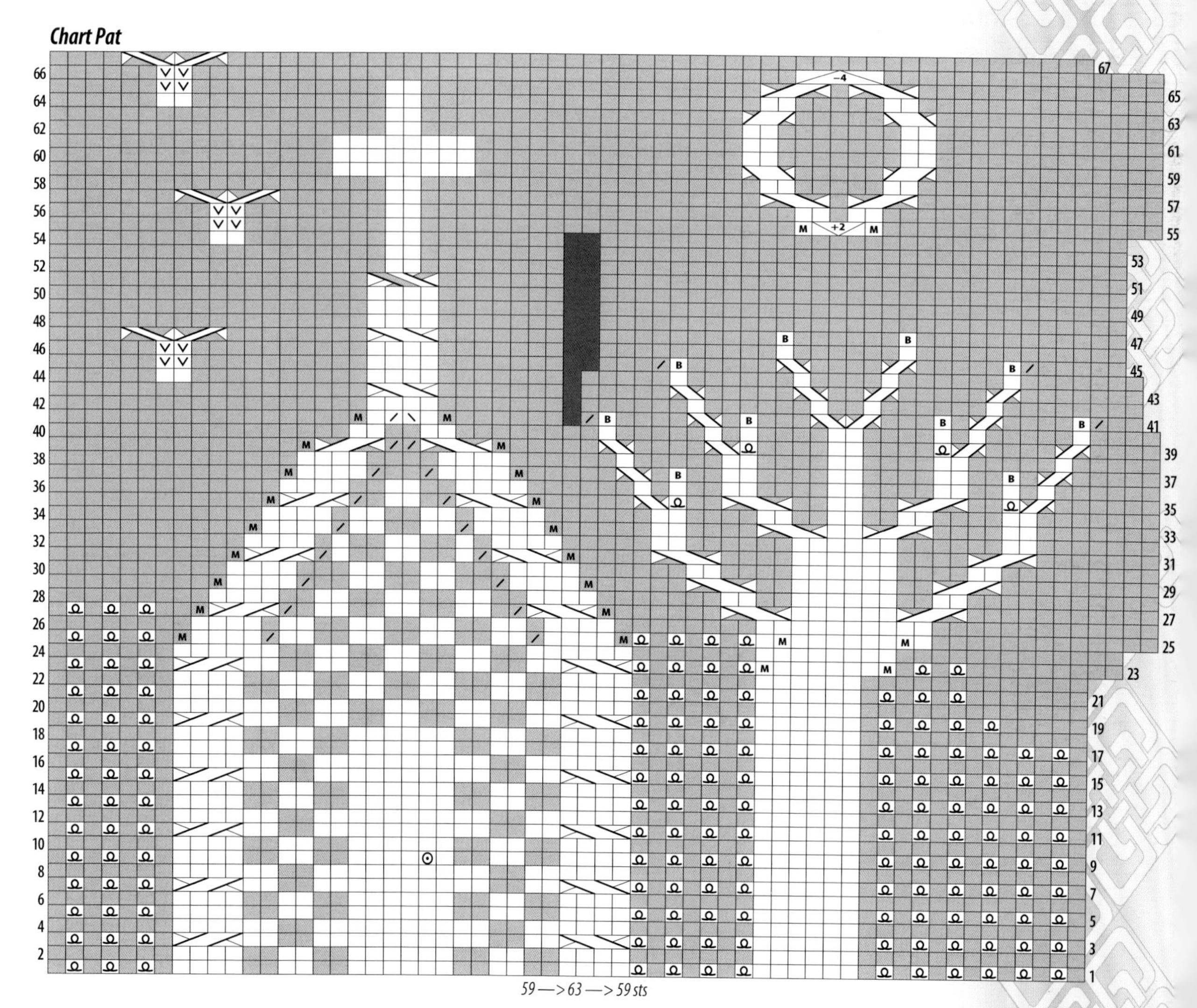

Hanna Burns

PORTLAND, OREGON

"My grandmother was my knitting inspiration and teacher. As a child I requested a pair of drop-seat pajamas for a stuffed animal, which she knit for me that very afternoon. I still carry them in the knitting bag she gave me. I love to knit small items such as dolls, stuffed animals, baby clothes, and fun socks. I am always searching for new and different projects that will challenge me.

"This square took shape after I read a series of articles in the newspaper about the mapping of the human genome. One article discussed the ethical dilemmas we may face as a result of recent and future discoveries. The pictures in the article looked just like Chart B. I have combined the two DNA strand-like patterns with the Trinity Stitch to represent the Holy Trinity in Christianity. The center panel seems an appropriate representation of the interconnectedness of God and science. I had a great deal of fun with this square and the ideas behind it. Chart B is worked to look as though it extends beyond the square.

Needles Size 5mm (US 8)

Extras Cable needle (cn)

Square

Cast on 62 sts. Work 3 ridges, end with a WS row. ***Beg Charts A, B, C and D: Next row*** (RS) K3, work 10 sts Chart A, 9 sts Chart B (beg with row 1), 4 sts Chart C, 10 sts Chart D, 4 sts Chart C, 9 sts Chart B (beg with row 17), 10 sts Chart A, k3. Keeping 3 sts each side in garter st (k every row), cont in chart pats as established until piece measures 11¼" from beg, end with a RS row. Work 3 ridges. Bind off.

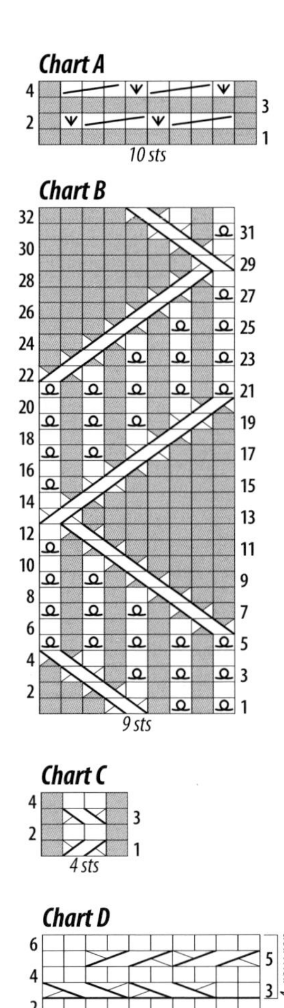

IN OTHER WORDS

TBL Through back loop
1/1 RC Sl 1 to cn, hold to back, k1; k1 from cn.
1/1 LC Sl 1 to cn, hold to front, k1; k1 from cn.
1/1 RPC Sl 1 to cn, hold to back, k1; p1 from cn.
1/1 LPC Sl 1 to cn, hold to front, p1; k1 from cn.
2/2 RC Sl 2 to cn, hold to back, k2; k2 from cn.
2/2 LC Sl 2 to cn, hold to front, k2; k2 from cn.

- K on RS, p on WS
- P on RS, k on WS
- K1 tbl
- [K1, p1, k1] in st
- P3tog
- 1/1 RC
- 1/1 LC
- 1/1 RPC
- 1/1 LPC
- 2/2 RC
- 2/2 LC

CHART A *OVER 10 STS*
Rows 1 and 3 (RS) Purl. ***2*** K1, [(k1, p1, k1) in next st, p3tog] twice, k1. ***4*** K1, [p3tog, (k1, p1, k1) in next st] twice, k1. Rep rows 1–4 for Chart A.

CHART B *OVER 9 STS*
Row 1 (RS) [K1 tbl, p1] twice, 1/1 LC, p3. ***2*** K2, 1/1 LPC, p1, [k1, p1] twice. ***3*** [K1 tbl, p1] 3 times, 1/1 LC, p1. ***4*** 1/1 LPC, p1, [k1, p1] 3 times. ***5*** [K1 tbl, p1] 4 times, k1 tbl. ***6*** P1, [k1, p1] 3 times, 1/1 LPC. ***7*** P1, 1/1 LPC, [p1, k1 tbl] 3 times. ***8*** P1, [k1, p1] twice, 1/1 LPC, k2. ***9*** P3, 1/1 LPC, [p1, k1 tbl] twice. ***10*** P1, k1, p1, 1/1 LPC, k4. ***11*** P5, 1/1 LPC, p1, k1 tbl. ***12*** P1, 1/1 LPC, k6. ***13*** P7, 1/1 RC. ***14*** P1, 1/1 RPC, k6. ***15*** P5, 1/1 RC, p1, k1 tbl. ***16*** P1, k1, p1, 1/1 RPC, k4. ***17*** P3, 1/1 RC, [p1, k1 tbl] twice. ***18*** P1, [k1, p1] twice, 1/1 RPC, k2. ***19*** P1, 1/1 RC, [p1, k1 tbl] 3 times. ***20*** P1, [k1, p1] 3 times, 1/1 RPC. ***21*** [K1 tbl, p1] 4 times, k1 tbl. ***22*** 1/1 RPC, p1, [k1, p1] 3 times. ***23*** [K1 tbl, p1] 3 times, 1/1 RPC, p1. ***24*** K2, 1/1 RPC, p1, [k1, p1] twice. ***25*** [K1 tbl, p1] twice, 1/1 RPC, p3. ***26*** K4, 1/1 RPC, p1, k1, p1. ***27*** K1 tbl, p1, 1/1 RPC, p5. ***28*** K6, 1/1 RPC, p1. ***29*** 1/1 LC, p7. ***30*** K6, 1/1 LPC, p1. ***31*** K1 tbl, p1, 1/1 LC, p5. ***32*** K4, 1/1 LPC, p1, k1, p1. Rep rows 1–32 for Chart B.

CHART C *OVER 4 STS*
Row 1 (RS) P1, 1/1 RC, p1. ***2 and 4*** K1, p2, k1. ***3*** P1, 1/1 LC, p1. Rep rows 1–4 for Chart C.

CHART D *OVER 10 STS*
Row 1 (RS) Knit. ***2*** Purl. ***3*** K2, [2/2 LC] twice. ***4 and 6*** Purl. ***5*** [2/2 RC] twice, k2.
Rep rows 3–6 for Chart D.

Pat Arrangement

3 sts garter st	10 sts Chart A	9 sts Chart B, beg row 17	4 sts Chart C	10 sts Chart D	4 sts Chart C	9 sts Chart B, beg row 1	10 sts Chart A	3 sts garter st

Ann Strong

OLYMPIA, WASHINGTON

"I live in a clearing in the woods. My house has many large windows and a sunroom where it is always a beautiful day. I get my inspiration from the patterns and colors of the outdoor environment, as well as from the produce displays in the market. I love pomegranates, especially their seediness and the contrast between the smooth exteriors and the seedy, bumpy insides. The Seed Wishbone stitch pattern (Charts B and C) reminds me of pomegranates and the Double Texture Cable (Chart A) illustrates the contrast between the inside and outside of the fruit."

Needles Size 4.5mm (US 7)

Extras Cable needle (cn)

Square

Cast on 60 sts. Work 3 ridges, inc 10 sts evenly across center 54 sts on last (WS) row—70 sts. ***Beg Charts A, B and C: Row 1*** (RS) K3, p4, work 8 sts Chart A, p4, k1 through back loop (tbl), p2, 8 sts Chart B, p1, 8 sts Chart C, p1, 8 sts Chart B, p2, k1 tbl, p4, 8 sts Chart A, p4, k3. ***2*** K7, 8 sts Chart A, k4, p1 tbl, k2, 8 sts Chart B, k1, 8 sts Chart C, k1, 8 sts Chart B, k2, p1 tbl, k4, 8 sts Chart A, k7. Cont in pats as established until 20 rows of Chart A have been worked 3 times, then work rows 1–13 once more. Work 3 ridges, dec 10 sts evenly across center 64 sts on first row—60 sts. Bind off.

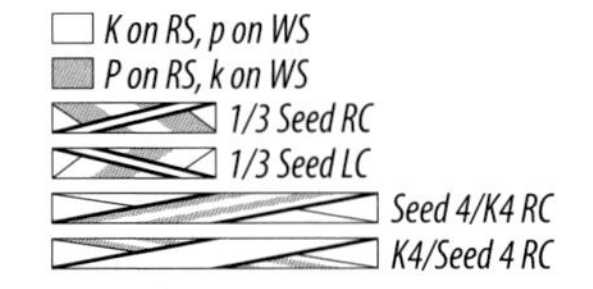

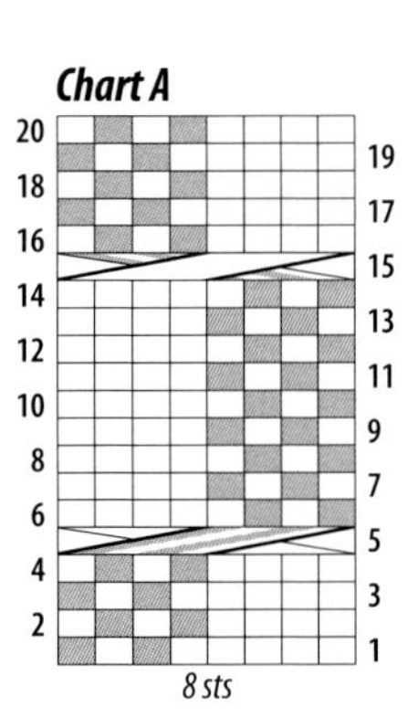

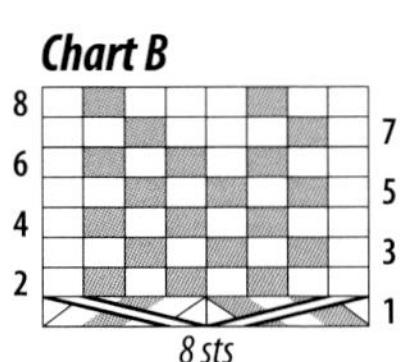

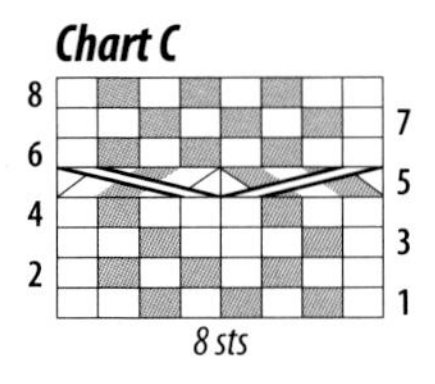

IN OTHER WORDS

1/3 SEED RC Sl 3 to cn, hold to back, k1; [p1, k1, p1] from cn.
1/3 SEED LC Sl 1 to cn, hold to front, k1, p1, k1; k1 from cn.
SEED 4/K4 RC Sl 4 to cn, hold to back, [k1, p1] twice; k4 from cn.
K4/SEED 4 RC Sl 4 to cn, hold to back, k4; [k1, p1] twice from cn.

CHART A *OVER 8 STS*
Rows 1 and 3 (RS) K5, p1, k1, p1. ***2, 4*** [P1, k1] twice, p4. ***5*** Seed 4/K4 RC. ***6, 8, 10, 12, 14*** P5, k1, p1, k1. ***7, 9, 11, 13*** [K1, p1] twice, k4. ***15*** K4/Seed 4 RC. ***16, 18, 20*** Rep row 2. ***17, 19*** Rep row 1. Rep rows 1–20 for Chart A.

CHART B *OVER 8 STS*
Row 1 (RS) 1/3 Seed RC, 1/3 Seed LC. ***2, 4, 6*** [P1, k1] 3 times, p2. ***3, 5*** [K1, p1] 3 times, k2. ***7*** K1, p1, k3, p1, k2. ***8*** P1, k1, p3, k1, p2. Rep rows 1–8 for Chart B.

CHART C *OVER 8 STS*
Row 1 (RS) [K1, p1] 3 times, k2. ***2*** [P1, k1] 3 times, p2. ***3*** K1, p1, k3, p1, k2. ***4*** P1, k1, p3, k1, p2. ***5*** 1/3 Seed RC, 1/3 Seed LC. ***6, 8*** Rep row 2. ***7*** Rep row 1. Rep rows 1–8 for Chart C.

Pat Arrangement

3 sts garter st	4 sts rev St st	8 sts Chart A	4 sts rev St st	1 twisted st	2 sts rev St st	8 sts Chart B	1 st rev St st	8 sts Chart C	1 st rev St st	8 sts Chart B	2 sts rev St st	1 twisted st	4 sts rev St st	8 sts Chart A	4 sts rev St st	3 sts garter st
								↑ center								

Janet Martin

CLARKSTON, MICHIGAN

"I began knitting when I was in college. I had tried to learn before and just couldn't get the hang of it. Knitting magazines filled with gorgeous sweaters enticed me to try my hand at knitting again. My mother sat down with me and then I finally got it! I haven't stopped knitting since.

"When I first read about the contest I started visualizing all sorts of cables and Celtic knots. Then I started thinking that Arans are associated with fishermen so I thought I'd put a fish on my square. (I may have been influenced by The Perfect Storm.*) I found a lot of appliqué and intarsia fish in my pattern books and magazines, but no Aran fish, so I sketched my own on graph paper. I caught my fish in a net and added a couple of ropes since no fisherman would go out in a boat without a rope."*

Needles Size 4mm (US 6)

Extras Cable needle (cn)

Note

See School, p. 60, for M1.

Square

Cast on 60 sts. Work 3 ridges, end with a WS row. ***Inc row*** (RS) [K6, M1, k7, M1] twice, k8, [M1, k7, M1, k6] twice—68 sts. ***Foundation row*** K4, p4, [k4, p2] 8 times, k4, p4, k4. ***Beg Charts A and B: Row 1*** (RS) K3, work 6 sts Chart A, work first 4 sts of Chart B, [work 6-st rep of Chart B] 7 times, then work last 4 sts of chart, work 6 sts Chart A, k3. Keeping first and last 3 sts in garter st (k every row), work charts as established through row 16 of Chart B. ***Beg Chart C: Next row*** (RS) Work 19 sts in pat, work Chart C over 30 sts, work to end. Work charts as established through row 48 of Chart C. Work Charts A and B as before for 12 more rows, ending with row 12 of Chart B. ***Next row*** (RS) K5, k2tog, k7, k2tog, [k5, k2tog] twice, k8, k2tog, [k5, k2tog] twice, k7, k2tog, k5—60 sts. Work 3 ridges. Bind off.

Chart A

4 2 3 1

6 sts

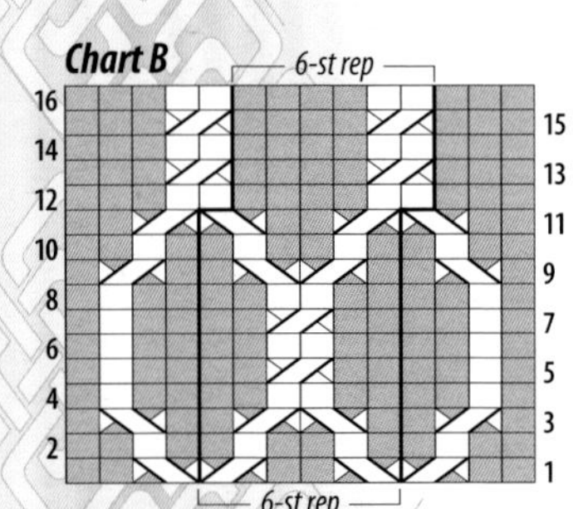

IN OTHER WORDS

CHART A OVER 6 STS

Row 1 (RS) P1, k4, p1. ***2 and 4*** K1, p4, k1. ***3*** P1, 2/2 LC, p1. Rep rows 1-4 for Chart A.

CHART B *MULTIPLE OF 6 STS, PLUS 2*

(***Note*** 6-st rep for Chart B shifts to the right one st after row 11, then back to left after row 16 so that it fits 'notched' rows of Chart C.)

Row 1 (RS) P2, 1/1 RPC, *1/1 LPC, p2, 1/1 RPC; rep from*, end 1/1 LPC, p2. ***2 and all WS rows*** K the knit sts and p the purl sts. ***3*** P1, 1/1 RPC, p1, *p1, 1/1 LPC, 1/1 RPC, p1; rep from*, end p1, 1/1 LPC, p1. ***5 and 7*** P1, k1, p2, *p2, 1/1 RC, p2; rep from*, end p2, k1, p1. ***9*** P1, 1/1 LPC, p1, *p1, 1/1 RPC, 1/1 LPC, p1; rep from*, end p1, 1/1 RPC, p1. ***11*** P2, 1/1 LPC, *1/1 RPC, p2, 1/1 LPC; rep from*, end 1/1 RPC, p2. ***13 and 15*** P3, *1/1 RC, p4; rep from*, end 1/1 RC, p3. ***16*** Rep row 2. Rep rows 1-16 for Chart B.

CHART C *OVER 30 TO 28 TO 30 STS*

Row 1 (RS) [1/1 LPC, p2, 1/1 RPC] 5 times. ***2*** K1, p1, k2, p1, k9, k2tog, k9, p1, k2, p1, k1—29 sts. ***3*** P1, 1/1 LPC, 1/ 1 RPC, p1, k17, p1, 1/1 LPC, 1/1 RPC, p1. ***4*** K2, p2, k2, [p1 tbl, k1] 9 times, k1, p2, k2. ***5*** P2, 1/1 RC, p2, [1/1 Twist LPC] 4 times, k1 tbl, [1/1 Twist RPC] 4 times, p2, 1/1 RC, p2. ***6*** K2, p2, k3, [p1 tbl, k1] 3 times, p3 tbl, [k1, p1 tbl] 3 times, k3, p2, k2. ***7*** P2, 1/1 RC, p3, [1/1 Twist LPC] 3 times, p1, k1 tbl, p1, [1/1 Twist RPC] 3 times, p3, 1/1 RC, p2. ***8*** K2, p2, k4, [p1 tbl, k1] 7 times, k3, p2, k2. ***9*** P1, 1/1 RPC, 1/1 LPC, p3, [1/1 Twist LPC] 3 times, k1 tbl, [1/1 Twist RPC] 3 times, p3, 1/1 RPC, 1/1 LPC, p1. ***10*** K1, p1, k2, p1, k4, [p1 tbl, k1] twice, p3 tbl, [k1, p1 tbl] twice, k4, p1, k2, p1, k1. ***11*** 1/1 RPC, p2, 1/1 LPC, p3, [1/1 Twist LPC] twice, p1, k1 tbl, p1, [1/1 Twist RPC} twice, p3, 1/1 RPC, p2, 1/1 LPC. ***12*** K4, p1, k4, [p1 tbl, k1] 5 times, k3,

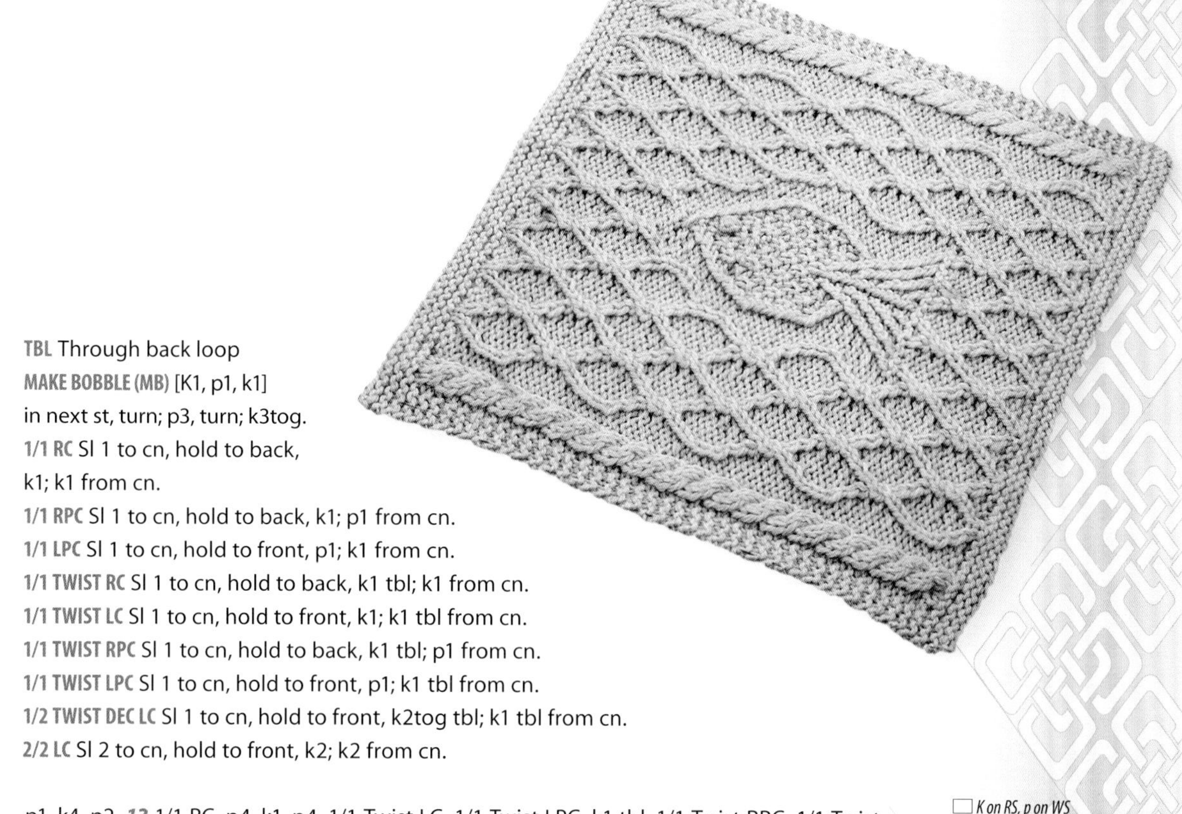

TBL Through back loop
MAKE BOBBLE (MB) [K1, p1, k1] in next st, turn; p3, turn; k3tog.
1/1 RC Sl 1 to cn, hold to back, k1; k1 from cn.
1/1 RPC Sl 1 to cn, hold to back, k1; p1 from cn.
1/1 LPC Sl 1 to cn, hold to front, p1; k1 from cn.
1/1 TWIST RC Sl 1 to cn, hold to back, k1 tbl; k1 from cn.
1/1 TWIST LC Sl 1 to cn, hold to front, k1; k1 tbl from cn.
1/1 TWIST RPC Sl 1 to cn, hold to back, k1 tbl; p1 from cn.
1/1 TWIST LPC Sl 1 to cn, hold to front, p1; k1 tbl from cn.
1/2 TWIST DEC LC Sl 1 to cn, hold to front, k2tog tbl; k1 tbl from cn.
2/2 LC Sl 2 to cn, hold to front, k2; k2 from cn.

p1, k4, p2. ***13*** 1/1 RC, p4, k1, p4, 1/1 Twist LC, 1/1 Twist LPC, k1 tbl, 1/1 Twist RPC, 1/1 Twist RC, p4, k1, p4. ***14*** K4, p1, k4, p2 tbl, k1, p3 tbl, k1, p2 tbl, k4, p1, k4, p2. ***15*** 1/1 RC, p4, k1, p3, 1/1 Twist RC, 1/1 Twist LPC, p1, k1 tbl, p1, 1/1 Twist RPC, 1/1 Twist LC, p3, k1, p4. ***16*** K4, p1, k3, p1 tbl, p1, [k1, p1 tbl] 3 times, k1, p1, p1 tbl, k3, p1, k4, p2. ***17*** 1/1 LPC, p2, 1/1 RPC, p2, 1/1 Twist RC, p1, k1, 1/1 Twist LPC, k1 tbl, 1/1 Twist RPC, k1, p1, 1/1 Twist LC, p2, 1/1 LPC, p2, 1/1 RPC. ***18*** K1, p1, k2, p1, k3, p1 tbl, [p1, k1] twice, p3 tbl, [k1, p1] twice, p1 tbl, k3, p1, k2, p1, k1. ***19*** P1, 1/1 LPC, 1/1 RPC, p3, k1 tbl, [p1, k1] 5 times, p1, k1 tbl, p3, 1/1 LPC, 1/1 RPC, p1. ***20 and 24*** K2, p2, k4, p1 tbl, [k1, p1] 5 times, k1, p1 tbl, k4, p2, k2. ***21*** P2, 1/1 RC, p4, k1 tbl, [k1, p1] 5 times, k1, k1 tbl, p4, 1/1 RC, p2. ***22*** K2, p2, k4, p1 tbl, [p1, k1] 5 times, p1, p1 tbl, k4, p2, k2. ***23*** P2, 1/1 RC, p4, k1 tbl, [p1, k1] 5 times, p1, k1 tbl, p4, 1/1 RC, p2. ***25*** P1, 1/1 RPC, 1/1 LPC, p3, k1 tbl, [k1, p1] 5 times, k1, k1 tbl, p3, 1/1 RPC, 1/1 LPC, p1. ***26*** K1, p1, k2, p1, k3, p1 tbl, [p1, k1] 5 times, p1, p1 tbl, k3, p1, k2, p1, k1. ***27*** 1/1 RPC, p2, 1/1 LPC, p2, k1 tbl, [p1, k1] 5 times, p1, k1 tbl, p2, 1/1 RPC, p2, 1/1 LPC. ***28*** K4, p1, k2, p1 tbl, [k1, p1] 5 times, k1, p1 tbl, k2, p1, k4, p2. ***29*** 1/1 RC, p4, k1, p2, 1/1 Twist LPC, [p1, k1] 4 times, p1, 1/1 Twist RPC, p2, k1, p4. ***30*** K4, p1, k3, p1 tbl, p9, p1 tbl, k3, p1, k4, p2. ***31*** 1/1 RC, p4, k1, p3, 1/1 Twist LPC, [p1, k1] 3 times, p1, 1/1 Twist RPC, p3, k1, p4. ***32*** K4, p2, k3, p1 tbl, p7, p1 tbl, k3, p2, k4, p2. ***33*** 1/1 LPC, p2, 1/1 RPC, 1/1 LPC, p2, 1/1 Twist LPC, p1, MB, p1, k1, p1, 1/1 Twist RPC, p2, 1/1 RPC, 1/1 LPC, p2, 1/1 RPC. ***34*** K1, p1, [k2, p1] twice, k3, p1 tbl, p5, p1 tbl, k3, p1, [k2, p1] twice, k1. ***35*** P1, 1/1 LPC, 1/1 RPC, p2, 1/1 LPC, p2, 1/1 Twist LPC, p1, k1, p1, 1/1 Twist RPC, p2, 1/1 RPC, p2, 1/1 LPC, 1/1 RPC, p1. ***36*** K2, p2, k4, p1, k3, p1 tbl, p3, p1 tbl, k3, p1, k4, p2, k2. ***37*** P2, 1/1 RC, p4, k1, p3, 1/1 Twist LPC, p1, 1/1 Twist RPC, p3, k1, p4, 1/1 RC, p2. ***38*** K2, p2, k4, p1, k4, p1 tbl, p1, p1 tbl, k4, p1, k4, p2, k2. ***39*** P2, 1/1 RC, p4, k1, p4, 1/2 Twist dec LC, p4, k1, p4, 1/1 RC, p2—28 sts. ***40*** K2, p2, k4, p2, k8, p2, k4, p2, k2. ***41*** P1, 1/1 RPC, 1/1 LPC, p2, 1/1 RPC, 1/1 LPC, p6, 1/1 RPC, 1/1 LPC, p2, 1/1 RPC, 1/1 LPC, p1. ***42*** K1, p1, [k2, p1] 3 times, M1 knit, k6, M1 knit, [p1, k2] 3 times, p1, k1—30 sts. ***43*** [1/1 RPC, p2, 1/1 LPC] 5 times. ***44, 46 and 48*** [K4, p2] 5 times. ***45 and 47*** [1/1 RC, p4] 5 times.

- K on RS, p on WS
- P on RS, k on WS
- K2tog on WS
- B Make Bobble (MB)
- M M1 Knit on WS
- K1 tbl on RS, p1 tbl on WS
- No sts exist in these areas of chart
- 1/1 RC
- 1/1 RPC
- 1/1 LPC
- 1/1 Twist RC
- 1/1 Twist LC
- 1/1 Twist RPC
- 1/1 Twist LPC
- 1/2 Twist dec LC
- 2/2 LC

Chart C

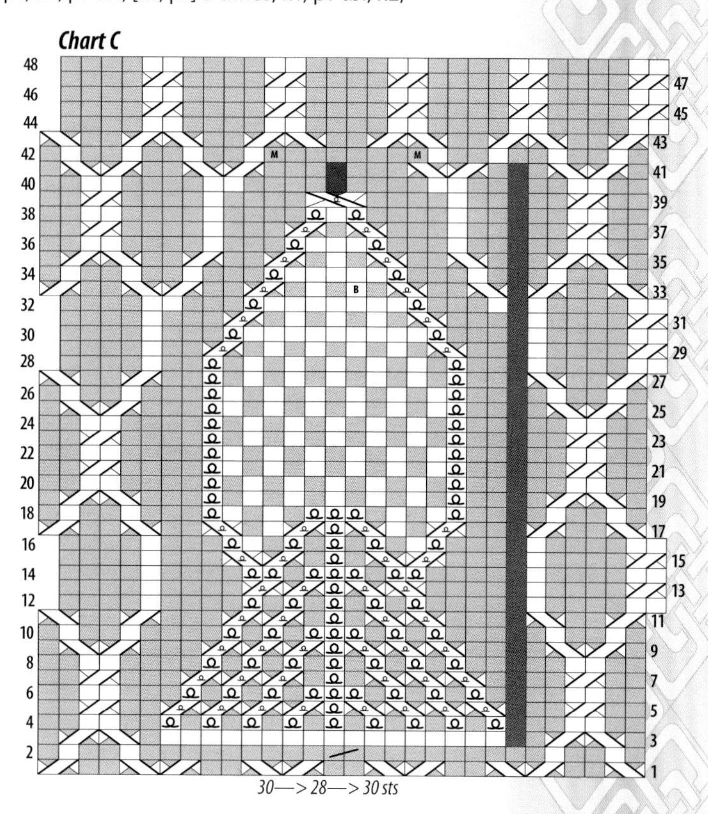

Ann McCauley

BOULDER, COLORADO

"I teach dance and movement at the Denver Center for the Performing Arts and the Boulder College of Massage Therapy. I have also taught many people to knit. When I commute by bus from Boulder to Denver I am so happy to be knitting!

"I design my own patterns; my designs reveal themselves to me as they are formed. Fortunately, as a dancer and knitter I enjoy the relationship between process and spontaneity. I have more knitting ideas and designs than I have time to knit.

"The Bobbledy Aran Square was inspired by my love of texture. Bobbles are so much fun. (Although the bobbles in the wavy panels might well be considered popcorn stitches, according to Barbara Walker, since they are worked without turning.) Barbara Walker is a mentor to me in knitting—I love her books and I could spend hours looking at them."

Needles Size 5mm (US 8)

Extras Cable needle (cn)

Note

See *School*, p. 60, for M1 Purl (M1P) and SK2P.

Square

Cast on 57 sts. Work 3 ridges, end with a WS row. ***Foundation row 1*** (RS) K3, 1/1 RC, p1, k2, p1, [k1, p1] 5 times, 1/1 RC, p15, 1/1 LC, p1, [k1, p1] 5 times, k2, p1, 1/1 LC, k3. ***2*** K3, k the knit sts and p the purl sts to last 3 sts, k3. ***Beg Charts: Row 1*** (RS) K3, work 2 sts Chart A, 14 sts Chart B, 2 sts Chart A, 15 sts Chart C, 2 sts Chart D, 14 sts Chart E, 2 sts Chart D, k3. Keeping first and last 3 sts in garter st (k every row), work charts as established until 24 rows of Chart B have been worked 3 times. ***Next 4 rows*** For Charts B and E only, [work rows 1–2] twice; for other charts work 4 rows even in pat. Work 3 ridges. Bind off.

TBL Through back loop

MAKE BOBBLE 1 (MB1) [K1, yo, k1, yo, k1] in next st, turn; p5, turn; k5, turn; p2tog, p1, p2tog, turn; SK2P.

MAKE BOBBLE 2 (MB2) [K1, p1 tbl] 3 times in next st, then pass 2nd, 3rd, 4th, 5th, and 6th st, one at a time, over first st and off needle.

1/1 RC Sl 1 to cn, hold to back, k1; k1 from cn.

1/1 LC Sl 1 to cn, hold to front, k1; k1 from cn.

1/1 RPC Sl 1 to cn, hold to back, k1; p1 from cn.

1/1 LPC Sl 1 to cn, hold to front, p1; k1 from cn.

2/2 RPC Sl 2 to cn, hold to back, k2; p2 from cn.

2/2 LPC Sl 2 to cn, hold to front, p2; k2 from cn.

2/2 PKRC Sl 2 to cn, hold to back, k2; [p1, k1] from cn.

2/2 KPLC Sl 2 to cn, hold to front, k1, p1; k2 from cn.

K on RS, p on WS
P on RS, k on WS
K1 tbl on RS, p1 tbl on WS
M1 Purl (M1P)
SK2P
Make Bobble 1 (MB1)
Make Bobble 2 (MB2)
1/1 RC
1/1 LC
1/1 RPC
1/1 LPC
2/2 RPC
2/2 LPC
2/2 PKRC
2/2 KPLC

Pat Arrangement

3 sts garter st	2 sts Chart D	14 sts Chart E	2 sts Chart D	15 sts Chart C	2 sts Chart A	14 sts Chart B	2 sts Chart A	3 sts garter st

IN OTHER WORDS

Chart A

2 1

2 sts

CHART A *OVER 2 STS*

Row 1 (RS) 1/1 RC. ***2*** P2. Rep rows 1 and 2 for Chart A.

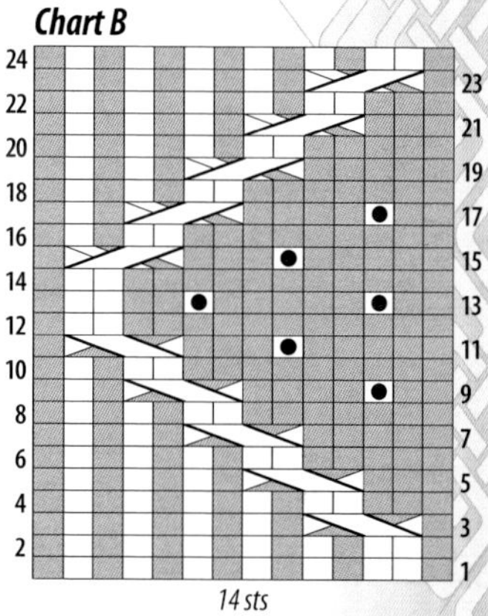

CHART B *OVER 14 STS*

Row 1 (RS) P1, k2, p1, [k1, p1] 5 times. ***2 and all WS rows*** K the knit sts and p the purl sts. ***3*** P1, 2/2 LPC, p1, [k1, p1] 4 times. ***5*** P3, 2/2 LPC, p1, [k1, p1] 3 times. ***7*** P5, 2/2 LPC, p1, [k1, p1] twice. ***9*** P2, MB2, p4, 2/2 LPC, p1, k1, p1. ***11*** P5, MB2, p3, 2/2 LPC, p1. ***13*** P2, MB2, p5, MB2, p2, k2, p1. ***15*** P5, MB2, p3, 2/2 PKRC, p1. ***17*** P2, MB2, p4, 2/2 PKRC, p1, k1, p1. ***19*** P5, 2/2 PKRC, p1, [k1, p1] twice. ***21*** P3, 2/2 PKRC, p1, [k1, p1] 3 times. ***23*** P1, 2/2 PKRC, p1, [k1, p1] 4 times. ***24*** Rep row 2. Rep rows 1–24 for Chart B.

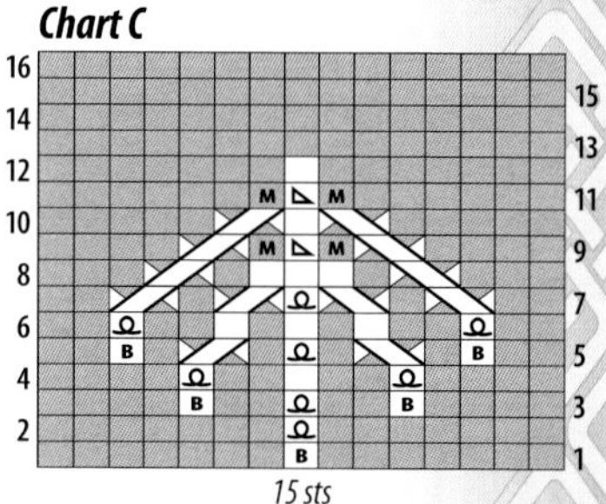

CHART C *OVER 15 STS*

Row 1 (RS) P7, MB1, p7. ***2*** K7, p1 tbl, k7. ***3*** P4, MB1, p2, k1 tbl, p2, MB1, p4. ***4*** K4, p1 tbl, k2, p1, k2, p1 tbl, k4. ***5*** P2, MB1, p1, 1/1 LPC, p1, k1 tbl, p1, 1/1 RPC, p1, MB1, p2. ***6*** K2, p1 tbl, k2, [p1, k1] 3 times, k1, p1 tbl, k2. ***7*** P2, 1/1 LPC, p1, 1/1 LPC, k1 tbl, 1/1 RPC, p1, 1/1 RPC, p2. ***8*** K3, 1/1 RPC, k1, p3, k1, 1/1 LPC, k3. ***9*** P4, 1/1 LPC, M1P, SK2P, M1P, 1/1 RPC, p4. ***10*** K5, 1/1 RPC, p1, 1/1 LPC, k5. ***11*** P6, M1P, SK2P, M1P, p6. ***12*** K7, p1, k7. ***13 and 15*** Purl. ***14 and 16*** Knit. Rep rows 1–16 for Chart C.

Chart D

2 1

2 sts

CHART D *OVER 2 STS*

Row 1 (RS) 1/1 LC. ***2*** P2. Rep rows 1 and 2 for Chart D.

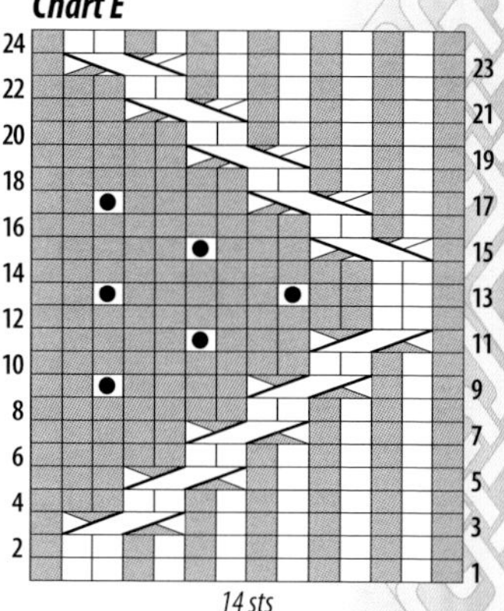

CHART E *OVER 14 STS*

Row 1 (RS) P1, [k1, p1] 5 times, k2, p1. ***2 and all WS rows*** K the knit sts and p the purl sts. ***3*** P1, [k1, p1] 4 times, 2/2 RPC, p1. ***5*** P1, [k1, p1] 3 times, 2/2 RPC, p3. ***7*** P1, [k1, p1] twice, 2/2 RPC, p5. ***9*** P1, k1, p1, 2/2 RPC, p4, MB2, p2. ***11*** P1, 2/2 RPC, p3, MB2, p5. ***13*** P1, k2, p2, MB2, p5, MB2, p2. ***15*** P1, 2/2 KPLC, p3, MB2, p5. ***17*** P1, k1, p1, 2/2 KPLC, p4, MB2, p2. ***19*** P1, [k1, p1] twice, 2/2 KPLC, p5. ***21*** P1, [k1, p1] 3 times, 2/2 KPLC, p3. ***23*** P1, [k1, p1] 4 times, 2/2 KPLC, p1. ***24*** Rep row 2. Rep rows 1-24 for Chart E.

Ginger Smith

LAKEWOOD, CALIFORNIA

"I learned to knit when I was 18 years old when a friend's mother offered to teach me. I chose a K1, P1 ribbed sweater, knit in black. After a 5-minute lesson I was on my own (my friend lived 400 miles away). Since I kept forgetting to bring the yarn back and forward into proper position for each stitch, that sweater was abandoned, never to surface again. Later, I bought a how-to book and the rest is history.

"I now teach knitting—and no, my students do not start with black yarn, or K1, P1 ribbing! I am certified by the Craft Yarn Council of America for knitting and crochet. Holding designated subjects credentials with the state of California, I teach at a local adult school and a yarn shop. I have taught for the Crochet Guild of America, and for other guilds. I have a line of knitting and crochet patterns, and I conduct an annual Knitting Camp in my area.

"At my camp in 1998, the featured project was a pillow cover of twisted stitches, in which panels are worked one at a time and joined as they are knitted. This design was based on an article in Knitter's *issue 16. I revisit this project in my square and I hope you enjoy it.*

"I live with my husband, Howard. Our two grown sons are married; one lives in Arizona and the other in North Dakota. My husband and younger son are knitters, too."

Needles Size 4.5mm (US 7) circular, 60cm (24") long

Extras Cable needle (cn)
Stitch markers and holders

Notes

1 See *School*, p. 60, for Make 1 knit (M1K) and Make 1 purl (M1P). **2** Square is made in columns which are joined to each other as they are worked.

Square

Cast on 59 sts. Work 3 ridges, end with a RS row. ***Inc row*** (WS) K3, p1, k2, p2, M1K, k1, p2, k2, M1P, [p1, k1] twice, p1, M1P, p1, k1, p2, k1, M1K, k2, p3, M1K, p2, k1, p1, k1, M1K, p2, k2, p1, M1P, k2, p2, k1, M1K, p1, k1, p2, k1, M1K, p2, k2, p1, M1P, k2, p1, k3—69 sts. ***Beg Chart A: Row 1*** (RS) Work 15 sts Chart A, place rem 54 sts on hold. Work until 10 rows of Chart A have been worked 7 times, then work rows 1-5 once more. Place marker (pm) and, with RS facing, pick up and k37 sts along left edge of column (one in each slipped st), place 5 sts from holder on LH needle, then work 5 sts of Chart B. Work Chart B until 75 rows have been worked (all the picked-up sts before the marker have been used). Pm and, with RS facing, pick up and k37 sts along left edge of column, place 29 sts from holder on LH needle, then work row 3 of Chart C. Work through chart row 16, then [work rows 1–16] 3 times, work rows 1–13 once more. Pm, pick up and k37 sts as before, work Chart B over next 5 sts from holder. Work Chart B as before. Pm, pick up and k37 sts as before, work Chart D over rem 15 sts. Work until 10 rows of Chart D have been worked 7 times, then work rows 1–5 once more. ***Next (dec) row*** (WS) Removing markers, k3, [p4, p2tog] 10 times, p3, k3—59 sts. Work 3 ridges. Bind off.

IN OTHER WORDS

2/1 LC Sl 2 to cn, hold to front, k1; k2 from cn.
2/1 RPC Sl 1 to cn, hold to back, k2; p1 from cn.
2/1 LPC Sl 2 to cn, hold to front, p1; k2 from cn.
2/2 RC Sl 2 to cn, hold to back, k2; k2 from cn.
2/2 LC Sl 2 to cn, hold to front, k2; k2 from cn.
2/2/2 LPC Sl 4 to cn, hold to front, k2, sl last 2 sts from cn to LH needle, hold cn to back, p2; k2 from cn.

Note On RS rows, sl sts knitwise with yarn in back. On WS rows, sl sts purlwise with yarn in front.

CHART A *OVER 15 STS*
Row 1 (RS) K4, p2, [k2, p2] twice, k1. ***2 and all WS rows*** Sl 1, [k2, p2] twice, k2, p1, k3. ***3*** K4, p2, 2/2/2 LPC, p2, k1. ***5, 7, 9*** Rep row 1. ***10*** Rep row 2. Rep rows 1–10 for Chart A.

CHART B *OVER 5 STS*
Row 1 (RS) Sl 1, k1, p1, k2. ***2*** Sl 1, k1, p1, k1, p2tog (1 chart st tog with 1 picked-up st). Rep rows 1 and 2 for Chart B.

CHART C *OVER 29 STS*
Row 1 (RS) Sl 1, k1, p2, 2/1 RPC, 2/1 LPC, [k1, p1] twice, 2/1 RPC, 2/1 LC, p4, 2/1 RPC, k2. ***2 and all WS rows*** Sl 1, k the knit sts and p the purl sts over 27 sts, p2tog. ***Row 3*** Sl 1, k1, p1, 2/1 RPC, p2, 2/1 LPC, k1, p1, 2/1 RPC, k1, p1, 2/1 LC, p2, 2/1 RPC, p1, k2. ***5*** Sl 1, k1, 2/1 RPC, p4, 2/1 LPC, 2/1 RPC, [k1, p1] twice, 2/1 LC, 2/1 RPC, p2, k2. ***7*** Sl 1, k3, p6, 2/2 RC, [k1, p1] 3 times, 2/2 RC, p3, k2. ***9*** Sl 1, k1, 2/1 LPC, p4, 2/1 RPC, 2/1 LC, [k1, p1] twice, 2/1 RPC, 2/1 LPC, p2, k2. ***11*** Sl 1, k1, p1, 2/1 LPC, p2, 2/1 RPC, k1, p1, 2/1 LC, k1, p1, 2/1 RPC, p2, 2/1 LPC, p1, k2. ***13*** Sl 1, k1, p2, 2/1 LPC, 2/1 RPC, [k1, p1] twice, 2/1 LC, 2/1 RPC, p4, 2/1 LPC, k2. ***15*** Sl 1, k1, p3, 2/2 LC, [k1, p1] 3 times, 2/2 LC, p6, k4. ***16*** Rep row 2. Rep rows 1–16 for Chart C.

CHART D *OVER 15 STS*
Row 1 (RS) Sl 1, p2, [k2, p2] twice, k4. ***2 and all WS rows*** K3, p1, [k2, p2] twice, k2, p2tog. ***3*** Sl 1, p2, 2/2/2 LPC, p2, k4. ***5, 7, 9*** Rep row 1. ***10*** Rep row 2. Rep rows 1–10 for Chart D.

K on RS, p on WS
P on RS, k on WS
On RS: sl st knitwise with yarn in back; On WS: sl st purlwise with yarn in front
P2tog (1 chart st tog with 1 picked-up st)
2/1 LC
2/1 RPC
2/1 LPC
2/2 RC
2/2 LC
2/2/2 LPC

Chart A

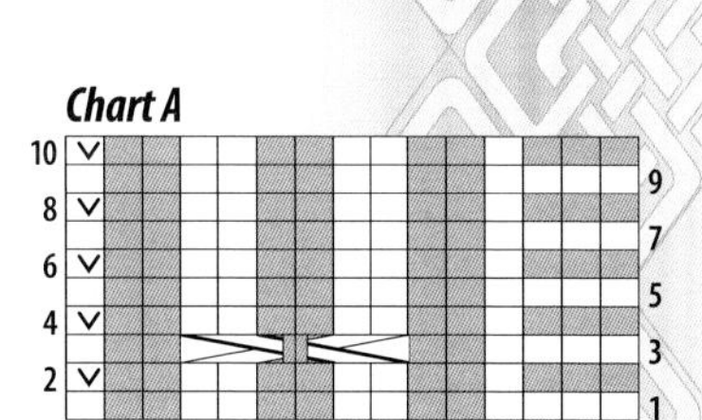

Chart B

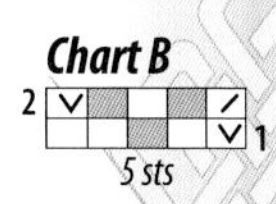

Chart C

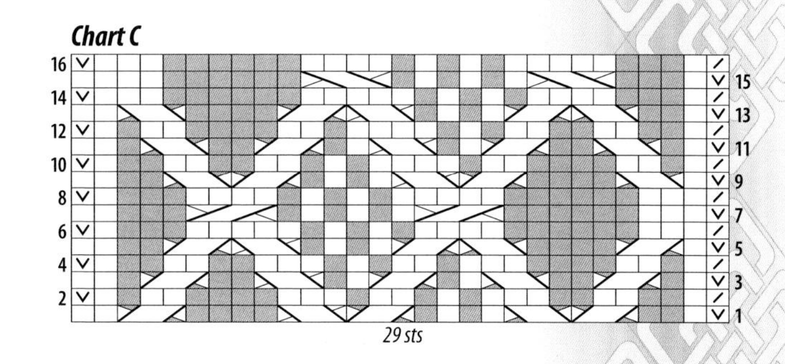

Chart D

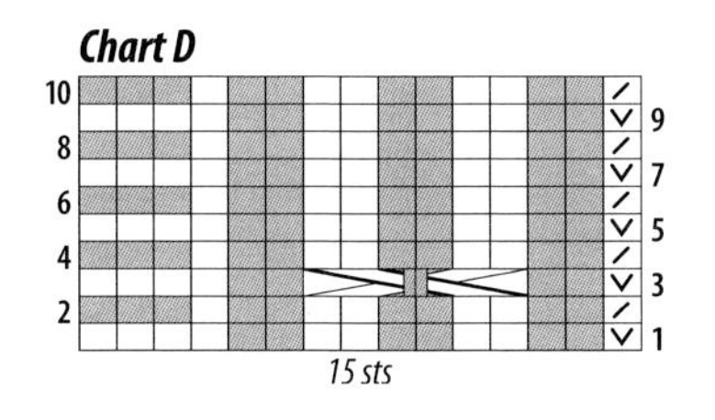

Pat Arrangement

15 sts Chart D	5 sts Chart B	29 sts Chart C, beg row 3	5 sts Chart B	15 sts Chart A

Patt Tanton Hewitt

PORTAGE, MICHIGAN

"I learned to knit in fifth grade when my younger sister was being taught to knit in her third grade class. She would come home and teach my brother and me, and with mom's help, we all learned. For me, it became a passion. I knitted pincushions, simple Barbie clothes, and eventually graduated to following patterns for mittens, stuffed animals, and sweaters.

"Although knitting is one of my great passions, I also love teaching, technology, and gardening. I have a wonderful husband and three children. A teacher for 28 years, I instructed emotionally impaired students for 18 years and second graders for the past 10 years.

"I knit for relaxation and during travel. I do not often follow a set pattern but take the best from several to make exactly what I want. I love to collect patterns that may someday be part of a project. This square is a combination of my favorites—cables, bobbles, and slip stitches."

Needles Size 4mm (US 6)
Two size 4mm (US 6) double-pointed needles (dpn)

Extras Cable needle (cn)

Note

See *School*, p. 60, for M1 purl (M1P) and ssk.

INC 1 K into front and back of st.
INC 2 K into front, back, and front of st.

Square

Cast on 61 sts. Work 3 ridges, working last row as foll: K3, [inc 1, k1] 13 times, inc 1, inc 2, inc 1, [k1, inc 1] 13 times, k3—91 sts. ***Beg Chart pats: Row 1*** (RS) K3, work 8 sts Chart A, 9 sts Chart B, 8 sts Chart A, 35 sts Chart C, 8 sts Chart D, 9 sts Chart E, 8 sts Chart D, k3. Keeping first and last 3 sts in garter st (k every row), work charts as established until 28 rows of Chart C have been worked 3 times, then work rows 1–4 once more. ***Next (dec) row*** (RS) K3, [k2tog, k1] 13 times, k2tog, k3tog, k2tog, [k1, k2tog] 13 times, k3—61 sts. Work 3 ridges. Bind off.

MAKE BOBBLE (MB) [P into front, back, front, back, front] of st, turn; k5, turn; p5, turn; k5, turn; bring yarn to back and pass 2nd, 3rd, 4th, and 5th st on LH needle, one at a time, over first st, then k st through back loop.
2/2 RC Sl 2 to cn, hold to back, k2; k2 from cn.
2/2 LC Sl 2 to cn, hold to front, k2; k2 from cn.
2/5/2 RC Sl 2 to dpn, sl 2 to 2nd dpn, hold to back of first dpn, sl 1 to cn, hold to front, sl 2 to 2nd dpn, hold to back, k2 keeping dpns in back and cn in front; return sts from first dpn to LH needle, p2 from 2nd dpn, k1 from cn, p2 from 2nd dpn, k2.
2/5/2 LC Sl 2 to dpn, sl 2 to 2nd dpn, hold to back of first dpn, sl 1 to cn, hold to front, sl 2 to 2nd dpn, hold to back, k2 keeping 2nd dpn in back and first dpn and cn in front; return sts from first dpn to LH needle, p2 from 2nd dpn, k1 from cn, p2 from 2nd dpn, k2.
4/3/4 RC Sl 4 to dpn, sl 1 to 2nd dpn, hold to back of first dpn, sl 1 to cn, hold to front, sl 1 to 2nd (back) dpn, k4 keeping dpns in back and cn in front; return 4 sts from first (middle) dpn to LH needle, p1 from 2nd dpn, k1 from cn, p1 from 2nd dpn, k4.
4/4/4 RC Sl 4 to dpn, sl 4 to 2nd dpn, hold to back of first dpn, k4 keeping both dpns to back; return sts from first (middle) dpn to LH needle, k4 from 2nd dpn, k4 from LH needle.
4/4/4 LC Sl 4 to dpn, hold to front, sl 4 to 2nd dpn, hold to back; with RH needle between dpns, k4 from LH needle, k4 from 2nd dpn (in back), k4 from first dpn (in front).

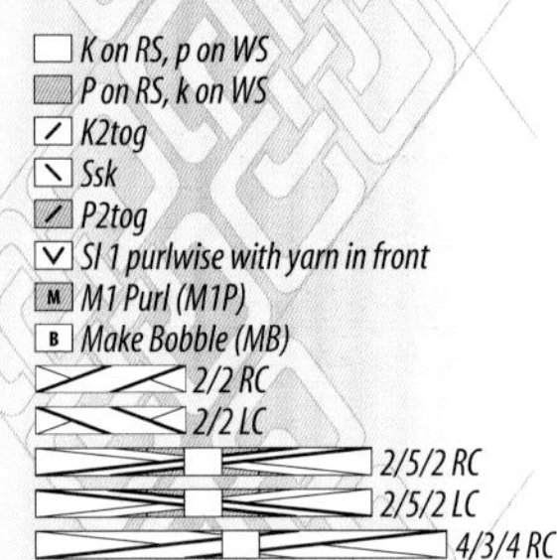

Pat Arrangement

3 sts garter st	8 sts Chart D	9 sts Chart E	8 sts Chart D	35-43-35 sts Chart C	8 sts Chart A	9 sts Chart B	8 sts Chart A	3 sts garter st

IN OTHER WORDS

Note Sl sts purlwise with yarn in front.

CHART A *OVER 8 STS*

Row 1 (RS) P2, k4, p2. ***2 and 4*** K2, p4, k2. ***3*** P2, 2/2 LC, p2. Rep rows 1–4 for Chart A.

CHART B *OVER 9 STS*

Row 1 (RS) Knit. ***2, 4, 6, 8*** P4, sl 1, p4. ***3*** 2/2 RC, k1, 2/2 LC. ***5*** K4, MB, k4. ***7*** K3, MB, k1, MB, k3. ***9, 11, 15, 17*** K2, p2, k1, p2, k2. ***10, 12, 14, 16, 18, 20*** P2, k2, sl 1, k2, p2. ***13 and 19*** 2/5/2 RC. ***21-28*** Rep rows 1-8. Rep rows 1–28 for Chart B.

CHART C *OVER 35 TO 43 TO 35 STS*

Row 1 (RS) *[K4, p2] twice, k4*, p1, k1, p1, work from *to*. ***2, 4, 6, 8*** *[P4, k2] twice, p4*, k1, sl 1, k1, work from *to*. ***3*** K4, p2, 2/2 LC, p2, k4, p1, k1, p1, k4, p2, 2/2 RC, p2, k4. ***5*** Rep row 1. ***7*** K4, p2, 2/2 LC, p2, 4/3/4 RC, p2, 2/2 RC, p2, k4. ***9*** *M1P, [k4, p2] twice, k4, M1P*, p1, k1, p1, work from *to* —39 sts. ***10*** K1, *[p4, k2] twice, p4*, k2, sl 1, k2, work from *to*, k1. ***11*** P1, M1P, k4, p2tog, 2/2 LC, p2tog, k4, M1P, p2, k1, p2, M1P, k4, p2tog, 2/2 RC, p2tog, k4, M1P, p1. ***12*** K2, *[p4, k1] twice, p4*, k3, sl 1, k3, work from *to*, k2. ***13*** P2, *M1P, k3, ssk, k4, k2tog, k3, M1P*, p3, k1, p3, work from *to*, p2. ***14*** K3, p12, k4, sl 1, k4, p12, k3. ***15*** P3, M1P, k4, 2/2 LC, k4, M1P, p4, k1, p4, M1P, k4, 2/2 RC, k4, M1P, p3—43 sts. ***16 and 18*** K4, p12, k5, sl 1, k5, p12, k4. ***17*** P4, 4/4/4 RC, p5, MB, p5, 4/4/4 LC, p4. ***19*** P2, p2tog, k4, 2/2 LC, k4, p2tog, p2, MB, k1, MB, p2, p2tog, k4, 2/2 RC, k4, p2tog, p2—39 sts. ***20*** Rep row 14. ***21*** P1, *p2tog, [k4, M1P] twice, k4, p2tog*, p2, k1, p2, work from *to*, p1. ***22*** Rep row 12. ***23*** P2tog, k4, M1P, p1, 2/2 LC, p1, M1P, k4, p2tog, p1, k1, p1, p2tog, k4, M1P, p1, 2/2 RC, p1, M1P, k4, p2tog. ***24*** Rep row 10. ***25*** K2tog, k3, [p2, k4] twice, p2tog, k1, p2tog, [k4, p2] twice, k3, ssk—35 sts. ***26-28*** Rep rows 6-8. Rep rows 1–28 for Chart C.

CHART D *OVER 8 STS*

Row 1 (RS) P2, k4, p2. ***2 and 4*** K2, p4, k2. ***3*** P2, 2/2 RC, p2. Rep rows 1–4 for Chart D.

CHART E *OVER 9 STS*

Work same as Chart B, except work 2/5/2 LC on rows 13 and 19.

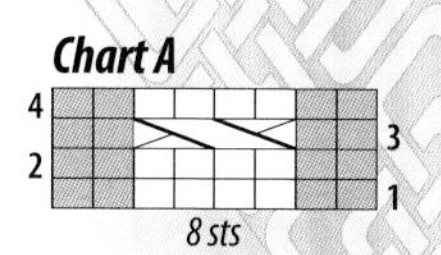

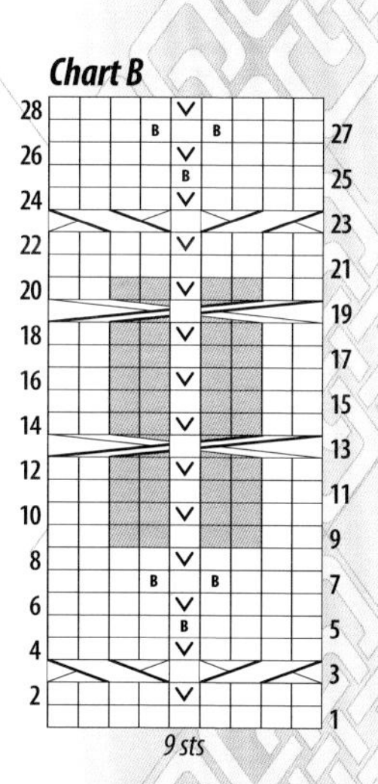

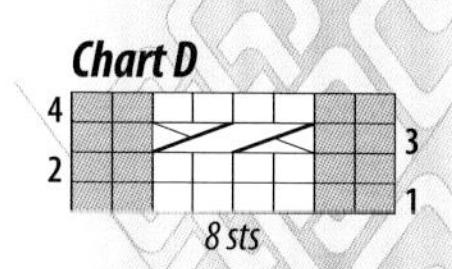

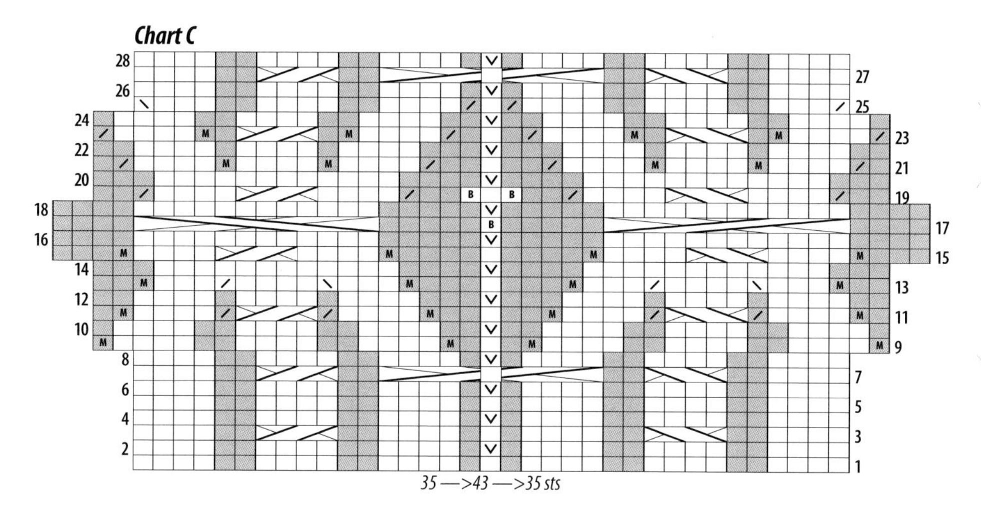

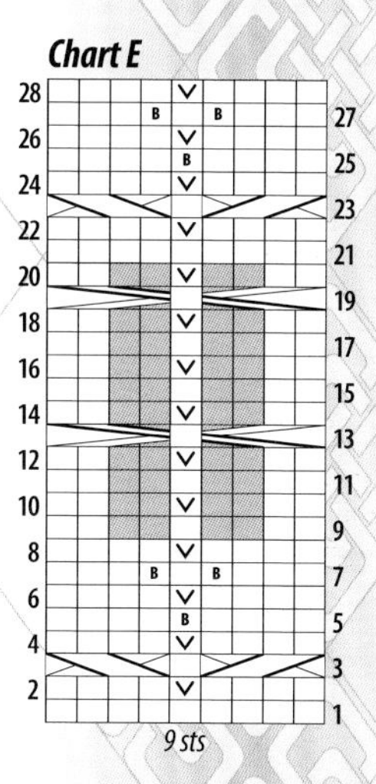

Barbara McIntire

MOUNTAINTOP, PENNSYLVANIA

"I've been knitting on and off for 25 years, but more seriously for the last five. My knitting focus is texture and cable patterns. I started a small knitting group several years ago because I enjoy the company of other knitters. I am a 'professional volunteer' for our public library, and I teach knitting for community education. My husband and I have two sons, 22 and 19 years old.

"The Saxon braid cable in Barbara Walker's book caught my attention several years ago and I wanted to make it the focal point of my square. The braided rib cable complements the Saxon braid to make a lovely example of Aran patterning."

Needles Size 5mm (US 8)

Extras Cable needle (cn)

Square

Cast on 54 sts. Work 3 ridges, inc 22 sts evenly across last (RS) row—76 sts. ***Foundation row*** (WS) K5, p2, k2, p2, k1, [p2, k2] twice, [p4, k4] 4 times, p4, [k2, p2] twice, k1, p2, k2, p2, k5. ***Beg Charts A, B, C and D: Row 1*** (RS) K3, work 17 sts Chart A, 4 sts Chart B, 28 sts Chart C, 4 sts Chart D, 17 sts Chart A, k3. Keeping first and last 3 sts in garter st (k every row), work charts as established until square measures approx 11½" from beg, end with a WS row. Work 3 ridges, dec 22 sts evenly across first row—54 sts. Bind off.

Pat Arrangement

3 sts garter st	17 sts Chart A	4 sts Chart D	28 sts Chart C	4 sts Chart B	17 sts Chart A	3 sts garter st

Chart D

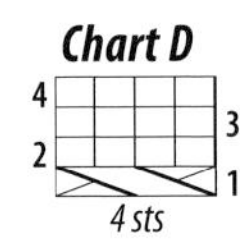

Chart C

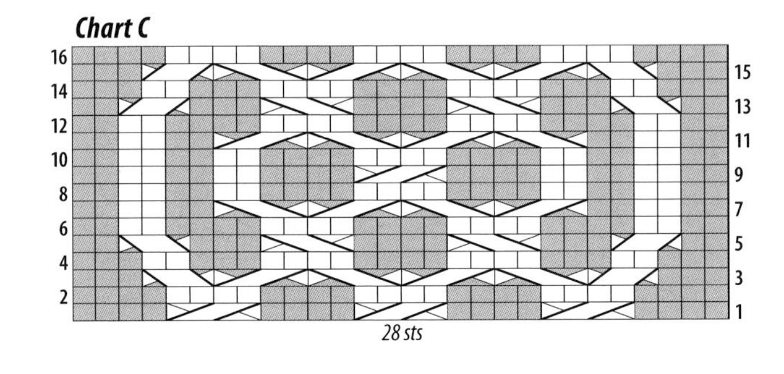

IN OTHER WORDS

2/1 RPC Sl 1 to cn, hold to back, k2; p1 from cn.
2/1 LPC Sl 2 to cn, hold to front, p1; k2 from cn.
2/2 RC Sl 2 to cn, hold to back, k2; k2 from cn.
2/2 LC Sl 2 to cn, hold to front, k2; k2 from cn.
2/2 RPC Sl 2 to cn, hold to back, k2; p2 from cn.
2/2 LPC Sl 2 to cn, hold to front, p2; k2 from cn.
2/1/2 RPC Sl 3 to cn, hold to back, k2; sl last st from cn to LH needle and p it; k2 from cn.
2/1/2 LPC Sl 3 to cn, hold to front, k2; sl last st from cn to LH needle and p it; k2 from cn.

CHART A *OVER 17 STS*
Row 1 (RS) P2, k2, p2, 2/1/2 RPC, p2, k2, p2. ***2 and all WS rows*** K the knit sts and p the purl sts. ***3*** P2, 2/1 LPC, 2/1 RPC, p1, 2/1 LPC, 2/1 RPC, p2. ***5*** P3, 2/2 RC, p3, 2/2 LC, p3. ***7*** P2, 2/1 RPC, 2/1 LPC, p1, 2/1 RPC, 2/1 LPC, p2. ***9*** P2, k2, p2, 2/1/2 LPC, p2, k2, p2. ***10-16*** Rep rows 2-8. Rep rows 1–16 for Chart A.

CHART B *OVER 4 STS*
Row 1 (RS) 2/2 RC. ***2 and 4*** P4. ***3*** K4. Rep rows 1–4 for Chart B.

CHART C *OVER 28 STS*
Row 1 (RS) P4, [2/2 RC, p4] 3 times. ***2 and all WS rows*** K the knit sts and p the purl sts. ***3*** P3, 2/1 RPC, [2/2 LPC, 2/2 RPC] twice, 2/1 LPC, p3. ***5*** P2, 2/1 RPC, p3, 2/2 LC, p4, 2/2 LC, p3, 2/1 LPC, p2. ***7*** P2, k2, p2, [2/2 RPC, 2/2 LPC] twice, p2, k2, p2. ***9*** [P2, k2] twice, p4, 2/2 RC, p4, [k2, p2] twice. ***11*** P2, k2, p2, [2/2 LPC, 2/2 RPC] twice, p2, k2, p2. ***13*** P2, 2/1 LPC, p3, 2/2 LC, p4, 2/2 LC, p3, 2/1 RPC, p2. ***15*** P3, 2/1 LPC, [2/2 RPC, 2/2 LPC] twice, 2/1 RPC, p3. ***16*** Rep row 2. Rep rows 1–16 for Chart C.

CHART D *OVER 4 STS*
Row 1 (RS) 2/2 LC. ***2 and 4*** P4. ***3*** K4. Rep rows 1–4 for Chart D.

K on RS, p on WS
P on RS, k on WS
2/1 RPC
2/1 LPC
2/2 RC
2/2 LC
2/2 RPC
2/2 LPC
2/1/2 RPC
2/1/2 LPC

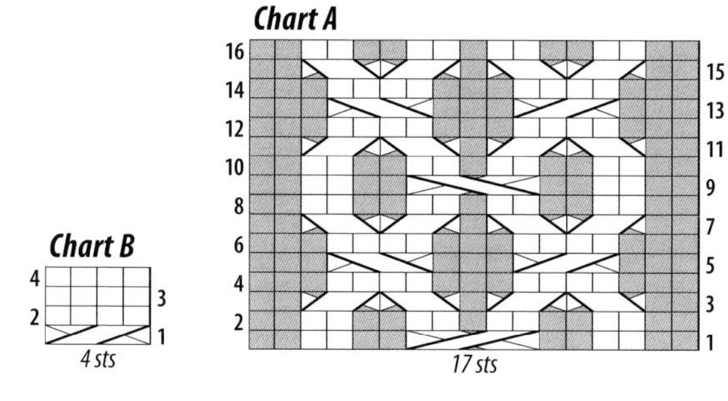

Ada Fenick

SETAUKET, NEW YORK

"My mother taught me to knit when I was eight. My first project was a purple garter stitch scarf. It probably would have been quite attractive if I could have kept the gauge even, but instead it had a nice wave to the border. Well, this turned me off knitting for a while, but I rediscovered it in college when I had a really boring math professor. I began to love it and was not embarrassed to knit in public (though I did sit in the back of the class).

"I live in Setauket, NY, with my husband and two sons. My husband, who is a (different) math professor, was horrified to learn of my knitting in math class. Now he seems to understand the importance of knitting in my life—it's my therapy!

"I designed my square in honor of a good college friend. Susan, who is Jewish, married Alan, who is Irish. The two cultures share (among other things) the symbol of the Tree of Life. The cables are taken from their wedding invitation."

Needles Size 4.5mm (US 7)

Extras Cable needle (cn)

Note

See *School*, p. 60 for ssk and SK2P.

Square

Cast on 53 sts. Work 3 ridges, end with a WS row. ***Beg Chart Pat: Row 1*** (RS) K3, work Chart Pat over 47 sts, k3—61 sts. Keeping first and last 3 sts in garter st (k every row), work chart as established through row 73—53 sts. Work 3 ridges. Bind off. ∩

LOOP CAST-ON

Uses To cast on a few sts for a buttonhole. Loops can slant either to the right or to the left. For right-slanting cast on, work the next row through the back loop.

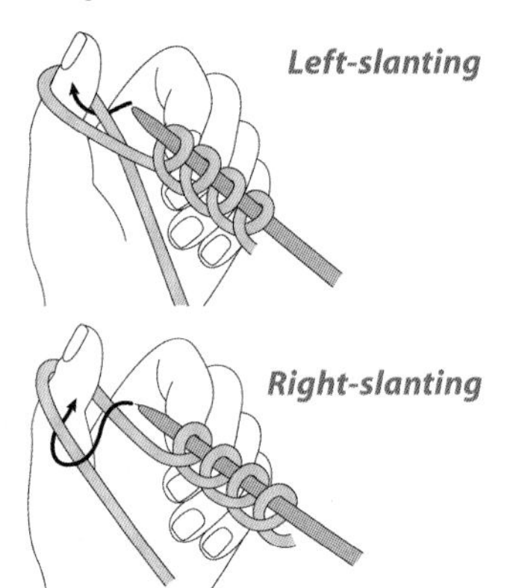

IN OTHER WORDS

P/K INC [P1, k1] into a st.
K/P INC [K1, p1] into a st.
INC 2 [K1, p1, k1] into a st.
MAKE BOBBLE (MB) [Yo, k1] 3 times in a st, turn, *sl 1 with yarn in front (wyif), p5, turn, sl 1 with yarn in back (wyib), k5, turn; rep from* once more, then [p2tog] 3 times, turn, SK2P.
DEC 3 (RIGHT) Wyib, sl 1 to RH needle; pass 2nd st on LH needle over first (center) st; sl center st to RH needle and pass 2nd st on RH needle over it; sl st back to LH needle and pass 2nd st over it; sl st to RH needle.
DEC 3 (LEFT) Wyib, sl 3 to RH needle; pass 2nd st on RH needle over first (center) st; sl st back to LH needle and pass 2nd st over it; sl st back to RH needle and pass 2nd st over it.
2/1 RC Sl 1 to cn, hold to back, k2; k1 from cn.
2/1 LC Sl 2 to cn, hold to front, k1; k2 from cn.
2/1 RPC Sl 1 to cn, hold to back, k2; p1 from cn.
2/1 LPC Sl 2 to cn, hold to front, p1; k2 from cn.
2/2 RC Sl 2 to cn, hold to back, k2; k2 from cn.
2/2 LC Sl 2 to cn, hold to front, k2; k2 from cn.
2/2 RPC Sl 2 to cn, hold to back, k2; p2 from cn.
2/2 LPC Sl 2 to cn, hold to front, p2; k2 from cn.
2/3 RPC Sl 3 to cn, hold to back, k2; p3 from cn.
2/3 LPC Sl 2 to cn, hold to front, p3; k2 from cn.

(continues on p. 52)

K on RS, p on WS
P on RS, k on WS
No sts exist in these areas of chart
P/K inc
K/P inc
Loop cast-on (CO 1)
Inc 2
K2tog
Ssk
SK2P
Make Bobble (MB)
P3 tog
Dec 3 (Right)
Dec 3 (Left)
2/1 RC
2/1 LC
2/1 RPC
2/1 LPC
2/2 RC
2/2 LC
2/2 RPC
2/2 LPC
2/3 RPC
2/3 LPC

Chart
47—>69Ð—>47 sts

Dagmara Berztiss

EGGENSTEIN, GERMANY

"As a child in Pittsburgh, one of the first things I learned to knit was Latvian mittens. Dr. Austra Zervins, an historian, taught me to use double-pointed needles, to carry yarn, and the meaning of Latvian symbols. These pagan symbols are geometric and mostly symmetric. In knitting they are represented in color rather than texture, but when I think of Aran knitting, I picture texture without color: twists, cables, and bobbles. Using texture, I wanted to represent my Latvian heritage in this square.

"The main element in this square is my interpretation of the Latvian moon cross. The moon cross is often associated with the god of war and warriors, and is also a protector of orphans. While my main goal was aesthetic—I like the shape and I thought it would translate well in texture—I also like that the symbol has meaning and various interpretations. The challenge was making a symmetric shape when gauge isn't! Graph paper was a big help. I chose a simple seed stitch border that wouldn't detract from the main design.

"I have a PhD in metallurgical engineering, but I have always been interested in arts and crafts. I like designing knitwear because it incorporates the analytical and the aesthetic. I also enjoy pottery and sculpture. I have recently begun knitting sculptural forms, wall hangings, and vessels in copper wire."

Needles Size 4.5mm (US 7)

Extras Cable needle (cn)

Note

See *School*, p. 60 for right-slanting Make 1 (M1R) and left-slanting Make 1 (M1L).

Seed st

OVER AN ODD NUMBER OF STS

Row 1 (RS) *K1, p1; rep from*, k1. ***2*** K the purl sts and p the knit sts. Rep row 2 for Seed st.

Square

Cast on 57 sts. Work 3 ridges, end with a RS row. ***Beg Seed st Border: Row 1*** (WS) K3, 1/1 RC, *p1, k1; rep from* to last 6 sts, p1, 1/1 LC, k3. ***2*** K3, p1, 1/1 LC, work 45 sts in Seed st, 1/1 RC, p1, k3. ***3*** K3, p1, k1, 1/1 RC, work 43 sts in Seed st, 1/1 LC, k1, p1, k3. ***4*** K3, p1, k1, p1, 1/1 LC, work 41 sts in Seed st, 1/1 RC, p1, k1, p1, k3. ***5*** K3, [p1, k1] twice, 1/1 RC, work 39 sts in Seed st, 1/1 LC, [k1, p1] twice, k3. ***6*** K3, *p1, k1; rep from* to last 4 sts, p1, k3. ***7*** K3, [p1, k1] twice, p21, p2tog, p20, [k1, p1] twice, k3—56 sts. ***8*** K3, [p1, k1] twice, p to last 7 sts, [k1, p1] twice, k3. ***9*** K3, [p1, k1] twice, p1, k to last 8 sts, [p1, k1] twice, p1, k3. ***Beg Chart: Row 1*** (RS) K3, [p1, k1] twice, p1, work Chart pat over 40 sts, [p1, k1] twice, p1, k3. Keeping 8 sts each side in pat as established (3 sts garter st and 5 sts Seed st), work Chart over center sts through chart row 60—56 sts. ***Next row*** (RS) K3, [p1, k1] twice, p21, p into front and back of next st, p20, [k1, p1] twice, k3—57 sts. ***Beg Seed st Border: Row 1*** (WS) K3, *p1, k1; rep from* to last 4 sts, p1, k3. ***2*** K3, [p1, k1] twice, 1/1 RC, work 39 sts in Seed st, 1/1 LC, [k1, p1] twice, k3. ***3*** K3, p1, k1, p1, 1/1 LC, work 41 sts in Seed st, 1/1 RC, p1, k1, p1, k3. ***4*** K3, p1, k1, 1/1 RC, work 43 sts in Seed st, 1/1 LC, k1, p1, k3. ***5*** K3, p1, 1/1 LC, work 45 sts in Seed st, 1/1 RC, p1, k3. ***6*** K3, 1/1 RC, work 47 sts in Seed st, 1/1 LC, k3. Work 3 ridges. Bind off. ∩

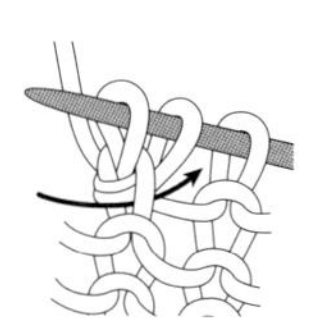

INC 2 K into back and front of st, then insert LH needle behind the vertical strand that runs between 2 sts just made (see illustration) and k strand tbl.

DEC 4 With yarn in front, sl 3, *pass 2nd st on RH needle over first (center) st, sl center st back to LH needle and pass 2nd st over it*, sl center st back to RH needle; rep from * to * once more, p center st.

1/1 RC (ON A RS ROW) K 2nd st on LH needle, then k first st, drop both sts off needle. **(ON A WS ROW)** P 2nd st on LH needle, then p first st, drop both sts off needle.

1/1 LC (ON A RS ROW) With RH needle behind work, k 2nd st through back loop (tbl), then k in front of first st, drop both sts off needle. **(ON A WS ROW)** With RH needle behind work, p 2nd st tbl, then p in front of first st, drop both sts off needle.

2/1 RPC Sl 1 to cn, hold to back, k2; p1 from cn.

2/1 LPC Sl 2 to cn, hold to front, p1; k2 from cn.

2/2 RC Sl 2 to cn, hold to back, k2; k2 from cn.

2/2 LC Sl 2 to cn, hold to front, k2; k2 from cn.

2/2 RPC Sl 2 to cn, hold to back, k2; p2 from cn.

2/2 LPC Sl 2 to cn, hold to front, p2; k2 from cn.

(continues on p. 54)

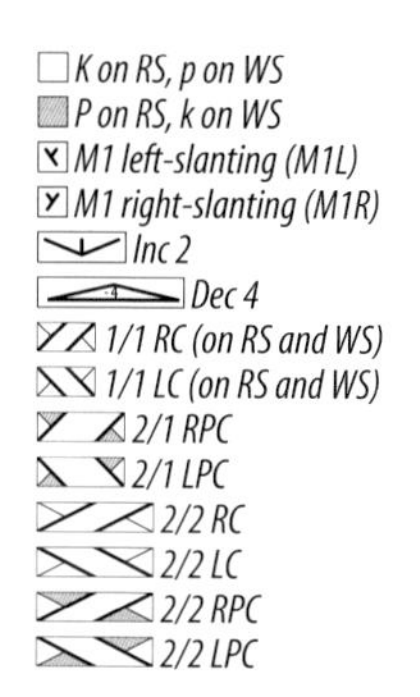

Chart

Susan Rainey

BROOKLYN PARK, MINNESOTA

"Knitting is my passion, and everyone who knows me knows it–my license plate is LV2KNIT (Love to Knit)!

"I have been knitting for over 35 years, avidly so for about 20. I love the feeling of accomplishment I get when I complete a really challenging project, like a Starmore Fair Isle. I look for designs that are classic, but with a unique spin. I tend to adapt every pattern I use, or I design my own. I am very proud to have sold a couple of my designs.

"As I thought about my entry for this contest, I kept thinking about what really symbolizes Aran knitting for me: the Irish Fisherman sweater. So I incorporated a mini sweater into my square. I chose a very classic set of stitches to make it instantly recognizable as a true Aran sweater.

"I think the mini-sweater idea would make a great afghan: knit squares with mini versions of your favorite handknit sweaters and combine them with stitch sampler squares. This would be a fun way to use up scrap yarn and showcase your favorite sweaters!"

Needles Sizes 3.5, 3.75, and 4mm (US 4, 5, and 6)

Extras Cable needle (cn)

Note

Square is worked first, then mini sweater is worked and sewn to square.

Square

With size 4mm (US 6) needles, cast on 57 sts. Work 3 ridges, inc 4 sts evenly along last (WS) row—61 sts. ***Beg center of square pat: Row 1*** (RS) K3, *p1, k1; rep from* to last 4 sts, p1, k3. ***2 and 3*** Rep row 1. ***4*** (WS) K3, p1, k1, p to last 5 sts, k1, p1, k3. ***5*** K3, p1, k to last 4 sts, p1, k3. Rep rows 4 and 5 until piece measures 11" from beg, end with pat row 4. Work rows 1–3 once. Work 3 ridges, dec 4 sts evenly across first row—57 sts. Bind off.

Mini Sweater

Body

With size 3.5mm (US 4) needles, cast on 39 sts. Work 5 rows in k1, p1 rib. ***Next row*** (WS) Purl, inc 4 sts evenly across—43 sts. Change to size 3.75mm (US 5) needles. ***Beg Charts A, B and C: Row 1*** (RS) Work Chart A over 5 sts, Chart B over 9 sts, Chart C over 15 sts, Chart B over 9 sts, Chart A over 5 sts. Cont in chart pats as established until piece measures 5" from beg, end with a WS row.

Shape armholes

Dec 1 st each side every RS row 3 times—37 sts. Work even until armhole measures 2¾", end with chart row 4.

Shape neck

Next row (RS) Work 13 sts, join 2nd ball of yarn and bind off center 11 sts, work to end. Working both sides at same time, bind off from each neck edge 2 sts twice—9 sts each side. Work 3 rows in St st. Bind off. Fold St st portion of each shoulder to WS and tack down.

Right Sleeve

With size 3.5mm (US 4) needles, cast on 11 sts. Work 5 rows in k1, p1 rib. ***Next row*** (WS) Purl, inc 1 st—12 sts. Change to size 3.75mm (US 5) needles. ***Beg Charts A and B: Row 1*** (RS) Work Chart A over 7 sts, work first 5 sts of Chart B. Cont in chart pats as established, inc 1 st at beg of RS rows (working incs into Chart A) every 4th row 4 times—16 sts. Work even until piece measures 3¾" from beg, end with a WS row.

Shape cap

Dec 1 st at beg of every RS row and end of every WS row until 3 sts rem. Bind off.

Left Sleeve

Work to correspond to right sleeve, reversing pats and shaping. Work chart pats as foll: ***Beg Charts A and B: Row 1*** (RS) Work *last* 5 sts of Chart B, work Chart A over 7 sts. Work incs at end of RS rows. Work sleeve cap decs at end of RS rows and beg of WS rows.

Finishing

Block pieces. Set in sleeves.

Neckband

With size 3.5mm (US 4) needles, pick up and k15 sts along neck edge. Work 3 rows in k1, p1 rib. Bind off purlwise.

Sl st sweater to square, using photo as guide. Leave neck and cuff edges open. ∩

IN OTHER WORDS

1/2 RC Sl 2 to cn, hold to back, k1; k2 from cn.
1/2 LC Sl 1 to cn, hold to front, k2; k1 from cn.
INC 2 [K1, yo, k1] in a st.

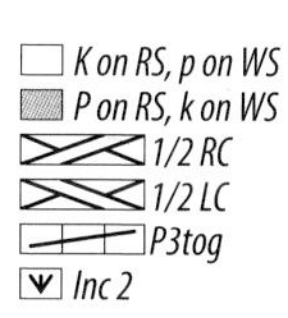

CHART A

OVER AN ODD # OF STS

Row 1 (RS) P1, *k1, p1; rep from*. **2** *K1, p1; rep from*, end k1. **3** Rep row 2. **4** Rep row 1. Rep rows 1–4 for Chart A.

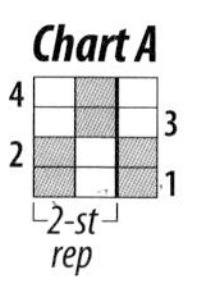

CHART B

OVER 9 STS

Row 1 (RS) P1, k7, p1. **2 and 4** K1, p7, k1. **3** P1, 1/2 RC, k1, 1/2 LC, p1. Rep rows 1–4 for Chart B.

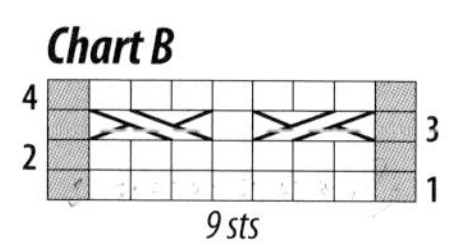

CHART C

OVER A MULTIPLE OF 4 STS PLUS 3

Rows 1 and 3 (RS) Purl. **2** *P3tog, inc 2; rep from*, end p3tog. **4** *Inc 2, p3tog; rep from*, end inc 2 in last st. Rep rows 1–4 for Chart C.

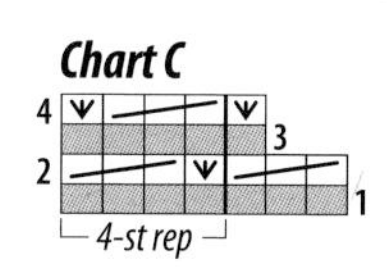

Continuations

ADA FENICK *continued from p. 46*

IN OTHER WORDS

CHART PAT *OVER 47 TO 69 TO 47 STS*

Row 1 (RS) *P/K Inc, K/P Inc, p5, P/K Inc, K/P Inc*, [p1, k1] twice, p25, rep from * to * once—55 sts. ***2*** *K1, p2, k7, p2, k1*, [Inc 2, p3tog] 6 times, [k1, p1] twice, k1, rep from * to * once. ***3*** P1, k2, p3, loop cast on 1 st (CO 1), Inc 2, p3, k2, [p1, k1] 5 times, p21, k2, p3, Inc 2, CO 1, p3, k2, p1—61 sts. ***4*** *K1, p2, k3, p4, k3, p2, k1*, [p3tog, Inc 2] 5 times, [p1, k1] 4 times, p1, rep from * to * once. ***5*** P1, 2/1 LPC, 2/2 RPC, k2, p3, k2, p2, [k1, p1] 6 times, p17, k2, p3, k2, 2/2 LPC, 2/1 RPC, p1. ***6*** K2, p4, k2, p2, k3, p2, k1, [Inc 2, p3tog] 4 times, [k1, p1] 6 times, k2, p2, k3, p2, k2, p4, k2. ***7*** P2, 2/2 RC, p2, k2, p3, k2, [p1, k1] 11 times, p9, k2, p3, k2, p2, 2/2 LC, p2. ***8*** K2, p4, k2, p2, k3, p2, k1, [p3tog, Inc 2] twice, [p1, k1] 11 times, p2, k3, p2, k2, p4, k2. ***9*** P1, 2/1 RPC, 2/2 LPC, k2, p3, k2, p2, [k1, p1] 10 times, p9, k2, p3, k2, 2/2 RPC, 2/1 LPC, p1. ***10*** *K1, p2, k3, p4, k3, p2, k1*, [Inc 2, p3tog] twice, [k1, p3] 3 times, [k1, p1] 4 times, k1, rep from * to * once. ***11*** P1, k2, p3, 2/2 LC, p3, k2, [p1, k1] 6 times, CO 1, p1, k1, p1, CO 1, k1, CO 1, p1, k1, p1, CO 1, k1, p1, k1, p9, k2, p3, 2/2 RC, p3, k2, p1—65 sts. ***12*** *K1, p2, k3, p4, k3, p2, k1*, p3tog, Inc 2, k4, p1, k1, p2, k1, p1, k1, p3, k1, p1, k1, p2, [k1, p1] 5 times, rep from * to * once. ***13*** *P1, 2/1 LPC, 2/2 RPC, 2/2 LPC, 2/1 RPC, p1*, [p1, k1] 5 times, 2/2 LPC, p1, k3, p1, 2/2 RPC, k1, p9, rep from * to * once. ***14*** *K2, p4, k4, p4, k2*, k9, p1, k2, p2, k1, p3, k1, p2, k2, [p1, k1] 5 times, rep from * to * once. ***15*** [P2, 2/2 RC, p2] twice, [k1, p1] 6 times, 2/1 LPC, k3, 2/1 RPC, p1, k1, p10, [p2, 2/2 LC, p2] twice. ***16*** *K2, p4, k4, p4, k2*, k10, p1, k2, p7, k2, [p1, k1] 5 times, p1, rep from * to * once. ***17*** *P1, 2/1 RPC, 2/2 LPC, 2/2 RPC, 2/1 LPC, p1*, [p1, k1] 6 times, p1, k7, p13, rep from * to * once. ***18*** *K1, p2, k3 p4, k3, p2, k1*, k13, p7, k7, [p1, k1] 3 times, rep from * to * once. ***19*** P1, k2, p3, 2/2 LC, p3, k2, [p1, k1] twice, p10, k7, p14, k2, p3, 2/2 RC, p3, k2, p1. ***20*** *K1, p2, k3, p4, k3, p2, k1*, k13, p7, k10, p1, k1, p1, rep from * to * once. ***21*** *P1, 2/1 LPC, 2/2 RPC, 2/2 LPC, 2/1 RPC, p1*, p13, k7, p13, rep from * to * once. ***22*** *K2, p4, k4, p4, k2*, k13, p7, k13, rep from * to * once. ***23*** [P2, 2/2 RC, p2] twice, p13, k7, p13, [p2, 2/2 LC, p2] twice. ***24*** Rep row 22. ***25*** *P1, 2/1 RPC, 2/2 LPC, 2/2 RPC, 2/1 LPC, p1*, p13, 2/1 RC, k1, 2/1 LC, p13, rep from * to * once. ***26*** *K1, p2, k3, p4, k3, p2, k1*, k13, CO 1, p7, CO 1, k13, rep from * to * once—67 sts. ***27*** P1, k2, p3, 2/2 LC, p3, k2, p13, 2/2 RC, k3, 2/2 LC, p13, k2, p3, 2/2 RC, p3, k2, p1. ***28*** K1, p2, k3, p4, k3, p2, k13, p11, k13, p2, k3, p4, k3, p2, k1. ***29*** P1, k2, p3, k2, 2/2 LPC, 2/1 RPC, p10, 2/3 RPC, k7, 2/3 LPC, p10, 2/1 LPC, 2/2 RPC, k2, p3, k2, p1. ***30*** K1, p2, k3, p2, k2, p4, k11, p2, k3, p7, k3, p2, k11, p4, k2, p2, k3, p2, k1. ***31*** P1, k2, p3, k2, p2, 2/2 RC, p8, 2/3 RPC, p3, k7, p3, 2/3 LPC, p8, 2/2 LC, p2, k2, p3, k2, p1. ***32*** K1, p2, k3, p2, k2, p4, k8, p2, k6, p7, k6, p2, k8, p4, k2, p2, k3, p2, k1. ***33*** P1, k2, p3, k2, 2/2 RPC, 2/1 LPC, p5, 2/2 RPC, p6, 2/1 RC, k1, 2/1 LC, p6, 2/2 LPC, p5, 2/1 RPC, 2/2 LPC, k2, p3, k2, p1. ***34*** K1, p2, k3, p4, k3, p2, k5, p2, k8, CO 1, p7, CO 1, k8, p2, k5, p2, k3, p4, k3, p2, k1—69 sts. ***35*** P1, k2, p3, Dec 3 (Right), p3, k2, p3, 2/2 RPC, p7, 2/2 RC, k3, 2/2 LC, p7, 2/2 LPC, p3, k2, p3, Dec 3 (Left), p3, k2, p1—63 sts. ***36*** K1, p2, k7, p2, k3, p2, k9, p11, k9, p2, k3, p2, k7, p2, k1. ***37*** P1, k2, p7, k2, p3, k2, p6, 2/3 RPC, k7, 2/3 LPC, p6, k2, p3, k2, p7, k2, p1. ***38*** K1, p2, k7, p2, k3, p2, k6, p2, k3, p7, k3, p2, k6, p2, k3, p2, k7, p2, k1. ***39*** P1, k2, p3, CO 1, Inc 2, p3, k2, p3, ssk, p4, 2/2 RPC, p3, k7, p3, 2/2 LPC, p4, k2tog, p3, k2, p3, Inc 2, CO 1, p3, k2, p1—67 sts. ***40*** K1, p2, k3, p4, k3, p2, k8, p2, k5, p7, k5, p2, k8, p2, k3, p4, k3, p2, k1. ***41*** P1, 2/1 LPC, 2/2 RPC, [k2, p3] twice, MB, p3, 2/1 RPC, p5, 2/1 RC, k1, 2/1 LC, p5, 2/1 LPC, p3, MB, [p3, k2] twice, 2/2 LPC, 2/1 RPC, p1. ***42*** K2, p4, k2, p2, k3, p2, k7, p2, k6, p7, k6, p2, k7, p2, k3, p2, k2, p4, k2. ***43*** P2, 2/2 RC, p2, k2, p3, k2, p7, k2, p4, 2/2 RPC, k3, 2/2 LPC, p4, k2, p7, k2, p3, k2, p2, 2/2 LC, p2. ***44*** K2, p4, k2, p2, k3, p2, k7, p2, k4, p2, k2, p3, k2, p2, k4, p2, k7, p2, k3, p2, k2, p4, k2. ***45*** P1, 2/1 RPC, 2/2 LPC, k2, p3, k2, p7, ssk, p3, 2/1 RPC, p2, k3, p2, 2/1 LPC, p3, k2tog, p7, k2, p3, k2, 2/2 RPC, 2/1 LPC, p1—65 sts. ***46*** K1, p2, k3, p4, k3, p2, k11, p2, k3, p3, k3, p2, k11, p2, k3, p4, k3, p2, k1. ***47*** P1, k2, p3, 2/2 LC, p3, k2, p7, MB, p3, k2, p3, 2/1 RC, p3, k2, p3, MB, p7, k2, p3, 2/2 RC, p3, k2, p1. ***48*** Rep row 46. ***49*** *P1, 2/1 LPC, 2/2 RPC, 2/2 LPC, 2/1 RPC, p1*, p10, ssk, p3, k3, p3, k2tog, p10, rep from * to * once—63 sts. ***50*** K2, p4, k4, p4, k16, p3, k16, p4, k4, p4, k2. ***51*** [P2, 2/2 RC, p2] twice, p10, MB, p3, SK2P, p3, MB, p10, [p2, 2/2 LC, p2] twice—61 sts. ***52*** K2, p4, k4, p4, k33, p4, k4, p4, k2. ***53*** *P1, 2/1 RPC, 2/2 LPC, 2/2 RPC, 2/1 LPC, p1*, p14, MB, p14, rep from * to * once. ***54*** K1, p2, k3, p4,

k3, p2, k31, p2, k3, p4, k3, p2, k1. ***55*** P1, k2, p3, 2/2 LC, p3, k2, p31, k2, p3, 2/2 RC, p3, k2, p1. ***56*** Rep row 54. ***57*** *P1, 2/1 LPC, 2/2 RPC, 2/2 LPC, 2/1 RPC, p1*, p9, [k1, p1] three times, p14, rep from * to * once. ***58*** K2, p4, k4, p4, k10, [p1, k1] 7 times, k9, p4, k4, p4, k2. ***59*** [P2, 2/2 RC, p2] twice, p9, [k1, p1] 9 times, p2, [p2, 2/2 LC, p2] twice. ***60*** K2, [p4, k4] twice, [p1, k1] 7 times, k15, p4, k4, p4, k2. ***61*** *P1, 2/1 RPC, 2/2 LPC, 2/2 RPC, 2/1 LPC, p1*, p15, [k1, p1] 6 times, p2, rep from * to * once. ***62*** K1, p2, k3, p4, k3, p2, k5, [p1, k1] 4 times, k18, p2, k3, p4, k3, p2, k1. ***63*** P1, k2, p3, 2/2 LC, p3, k2, p31, k2, p3, 2/2 RC, p3, k2, p1. ***64*** K1, p2, k3, p4, k3, p2, k31, p2, k3, p4, k3, p2, k1. ***65*** P1, k2, p3, k2, 2/2 LPC, 2/1 RPC, p31, 2/1 LPC, 2/2 RPC, k2, p3, k2, p1. ***66*** K1, p2, k3, p2, k2, p4, k16, [p1, k1] 3 times, k11, p4, k2, p2, k3, p2, k1. ***67*** P1, k2, p3, k2, p2, 2/2 RC, p7, [k1, p1] 7 times, p12, 2/2 LC, p2, k2, p3, k2, p1. ***68*** K1, p2, k3, p2, k2, p4, k12, [p1, k1] 8 times, k5, p4, k2, p2, k3, p2, k1. ***69*** P1, k2, p3, k2, 2/2 RPC, 2/1 LPC, p4, [k1, p1] 8 times, p11, 2/1 RPC, 2/2 LPC, k2, p3, k2, p1. ***70*** K1, p2, k3, p4, k3, p2, k17, [p1, k1] 6 times, k2, p2, k3, p4, k3, p2, k1. ***71*** P1, k2, p3, Dec 3 (Right), p3, k2, p8, k1, p1, k1, p20, k2, p3, Dec 3 (Left), p3, k2, p1—55 sts. ***72*** K1, p2, k7, p2, k31, p2, k7, p2, k1. ***73*** *K2tog, ssk, p5, k2tog, ssk*, p29, rep from * to * once—47 sts.

DAGMARA BERZTISS *continued from p. 49*

IN OTHER WORDS

CHART *OVER 40 TO 56 TO 40 STS*

Row 1 (RS) P11, [p4, M1R, Inc 2, M1L, p4] twice, p11—48 sts. ***2*** K11, [k4, p2, k1, p2, k4] twice, k11. ***3*** P13, 2/2 RPC, p1, 2/1 LPC, p6, 2/1 RPC, p1, 2/2 LPC, p13. ***4 and all WS rows (except 12, 14, 28, 34, 38, 48 and 60)*** K the knit sts and p the purl sts. ***5*** P10, [p2, 2/1 RPC, p4, 2/1 LPC, p2] twice, p10. ***7*** P10, [p1, 2/1 RPC, p6, 2/1 LPC, p1] twice, p10. ***9*** P10, [p1, 2/1 LPC, p6, 2/1 RPC, p1] twice, p10. ***11*** P12, 2/2 LPC, p4, 1/1 RC, p4, 1/1 LC, p4, 2/2 RPC, p12. ***12*** (WS) K14, p2, k16, p2, k14. ***13*** P6, M1R, Inc 2, M1L, p7, 2/2 LPC, p12, 2/2 RPC, p7, M1R, Inc 2, M1L, p6—56 sts. ***14*** (WS) K6, p2, k1, p2, k9, p2, k12, p2, k9, p2, k1, p2, k6. ***15*** P4, 2/2 RPC, p1, 2/2 LPC, p7, 2/2 LPC, p8, 2/2 RPC, p7, 2/2 RPC, p1, 2/2 LPC, p4. ***17*** P3, 2/1 RPC, p5, 2/2 LPC, p7, 2/2 LPC, p4, 2/2 RPC, p7, 2/2 RPC, p5, 2/1 LPC, p3. ***19*** P2, 2/1 RPC, p8, 2/2 LPC, p7, 2/2 LPC, 2/2 RPC, p7, 2/2 RPC, p8, 2/1 LPC, p2. ***21*** P2, 2/1 LPC, p10, 2/2 LPC, p7, 2/2 LC, p7, 2/2 RPC, p10, 2/1 RPC, p2. ***23*** P3, 2/1 LPC, p4, 1/1 RC, p5, 2/1 LPC, p6, 2/2 LC, p6, 2/1 RPC, p5, 1/1 LC, p4, 2/1 RPC, p3. ***25*** P4, 2/2 LPC, p1, 2/1 RPC, p6, [2/1 LPC, p4, 2/1 RPC] twice, p6, 2/1 LPC, p1, 2/2 RPC, p4. ***27*** P6, Dec 4, p7, [p1, 2/2 LPC, 2/2 RPC, p1] twice, p7, Dec 4, p6—48 sts. ***28*** (WS) K17, p4, k6, p4, k17. ***29 and 31*** P17, 2/2 LC, p6, 2/2 RC, p17. ***33*** P6, M1R, Inc 2, M1L, p7, [p1, 2/2 RPC, 2/2 LPC, p1] twice, p7, M1R, Inc 2, M1L, p6—56 sts. ***34*** (WS) K6, p2, k1, p2, k8, p2, k4, p2, k2, p2, k4, p2, k8, p2, k1, p2, k6. ***35*** P4, 2/2 RPC, p1, 2/1 LPC, p6, [2/1 RPC, p4, 2/1 LPC] twice, p6, 2/1 RPC, p1, 2/2 LPC, p4. ***37*** P3, 2/1 RPC, p4, 1/1 LC, p5, 2/1 RPC, p6, 2/2 RC, p6, 2/1 LPC, p5, 1/1 RC, p4, 2/1 LPC, p3. ***38*** (WS) K3, p2, k12, p2, k7, p4, k7, p2, k12, p2, k3. ***39*** P2, 2/1 RPC, p10, 2/2 RPC, p7, 2/2 RC, p7, 2/2 LPC, p10, 2/1 LPC, p2. ***41*** P2, 2/1 LPC, p8, 2/2 RPC, p7, 2/2 RPC, 2/2 LPC, p7, 2/2 LPC, p8, 2/1 RPC, p2. ***43*** P3, 2/1 LPC, p5, 2/2 RPC, p7, 2/2 RPC, p4, 2/2 LPC, p7, 2/2 LPC, p5, 2/1 RPC, p3. ***45*** P4, 2/2 LPC, p1, 2/2 RPC, p7, 2/2 RPC, p8, 2/2 LPC, p7, 2/2 LPC, p1, 2/2 RPC, p4. ***47*** P6, Dec 4, p7, 2/2 RPC, p12, 2/2 LPC, p7, Dec 4, p6—48 sts. ***48*** (WS) K14, p2, k16, p2, k14. ***49*** P12, 2/2 RPC, p4, 1/1 LC, p4, 1/1 RC, p4, 2/2 LPC, p12. ***51*** P10, [p1, 2/1 RPC, p6, 2/1 LPC, p1] twice, p10. ***53*** P10, [p1, 2/1 LPC, p6, 2/1 RPC, p1] twice, p10. ***55*** P10, [p2, 2/1 LPC, p4, 2/1 RPC, p2] twice, p10. ***57*** P13, 2/2 LPC, p1, 2/1 RPC, p6, 2/1 LPC, p1, 2/2 RPC, p13. ***59*** P11, [p4, Dec 4, p4] twice, p11—40 sts. ***60*** Knit.

BETTY SALPEKAR *continued from p. 25*

IN OTHER WORDS

2/1 RPC (on RS) Sl 1 to cn, hold to back, k2; p1 from cn.
(on WS) Sl 2 to cn, hold to back, k1; p2 from cn.
2/1 LPC (on RS) Sl 2 to cn, hold to front, p1; k2 from cn.
(on WS) Sl 1 to cn, hold to front, p2; k1 from cn.
2/2 RC Sl 2 to cn, hold to back, k2; k2 from cn.
2/2 LC Sl 2 to cn, hold to front, k2; k2 from cn.
2/2 RPC (on RS or WS) Sl 2 to cn, hold to back, k2; p2 from cn.
2/2 LPC (on RS or WS) Sl 2 to cn, hold to front, p2; k2 from cn.

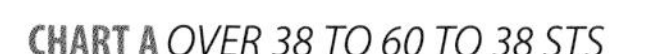

CHART A *OVER 38 TO 60 TO 38 STS*

Rows 1 and 3 (WS) Knit. ***2*** Purl. ***4*** P6, work Special Instruction A (SI-A), p6, SI-B, p6, SI-A, p6—44 sts. ***5*** (WS) K5, 2/1 LPC, k2, p2, k4, 2/2 LPC, k4, 2/2 RPC, k4, p2, k2, 2/1 RPC, k5. ***6*** P4, 2/1 RPC, p3, 2/1 LPC, p2, 2/1 RPC, p8, 2/1 LPC, p2, 2/1 RPC, p3, 2/1 LPC, p4. ***7*** K the knit sts and p the purl sts. ***8*** P3, 2/1 RPC, p1, *p1, SI-C, p3, 2/1 LPC, 2/1 RPC, p3, SI-C, p1*, p2, work from * to * once, p1, 2/1 LPC, p3—60 sts. ***9*** K3, p2, k2, [ssp, p2, p2tog, k3, p4, k3, ssp, p2, p2tog, k2] twice, p2, k3—52 sts. ***10*** P2, 2/1 RPC, p2, [k2, 2/1 LPC, p2, 2/2 RC, p2, 2/1 RPC, k2, p2] twice, 2/1 LPC, p2. ***11, 13, 15, 17, 19, 21*** Rep row 7. ***12*** P2, k2, p3, *k2, p1, [2/1 LPC, 2/1 RPC] twice, p1, k2*, p2, work from * to * once, p3, k2, p2. ***14*** P2, k2, p3, *k2, [p2, 2/2 LC] twice, p2, k2*, p2, work from * to * once, p3, k2, p2. ***16*** P2, k2, p3, *[2/1 LPC, 2/1 RPC] 3 times*, p2, work from * to * once, p3, k2, p2. ***18*** P2, k2, p4, [(2/2 RC, p2) 3 times, p2] twice, k2, p2. ***20*** P2, 2/1 LPC, [p2, (2/1 RPC, 2/1 LPC) 3 times] twice, p2, 2/1 RPC, p2. ***22*** P3, [2/1 LPC, 2/1 RPC, p2, (2/2 LC, p2) twice] twice, 2/1 LPC, 2/1 RPC, p3. ***23*** K4, [p4, k3, p2, SI-D, p2, k3] twice, p4, k4—48 sts. ***24*** P4, [2/2 LC, p2, 2/1 RPC, p4, 2/1 LPC, p2] twice, 2/2 LC, p4. ***25, 27, 29, 31*** Rep row 7. ***26*** P2, 2/2 RPC, [2/1 LPC, 2/1 RPC, p6, 2/1 LPC, 2/1 RPC] twice, 2/2 LPC, p2. ***28*** P2, k2, p3, *2/2 RC, p8, 2/2 RC*, p2, work from * to * once, p3, k2, p2. ***30*** P2, 2/2 LPC, [2/1 RPC, 2/1 LPC, p6, 2/1 RPC, 2/1 LPC] twice, 2/2 RPC, p2. ***32*** P4, [2/2 LC, p2, 2/1 LPC, p4, 2/1 RPC, p2] twice, 2/2 LC, p4. ***33*** K4, [p4, k3, p2, SI-E, p2, k3] twice, p4, k4—52 sts. ***34*** P3, [2/1 RPC, 2/1 LPC, p2, (2/2 LC, p2) twice] twice, 2/1 RPC, 2/1 LPC, p3. ***35, 37, 39, 41, 43, 45, 47*** Rep row 7. ***36*** P2, 2/1 RPC, [p2, (2/1 LPC, 2/1 RPC) 3 times] twice, p2, 2/1 LPC, p2. ***38*** Rep row 18. ***40*** P2, k2, p3, *[2/1 RPC, 2/1 LPC] 3 times*, p2, work from * to * once, p3, k2, p2. ***42*** Rep row 14. ***44*** P2, k2, p3, [k2, p1, (2/1 RPC, 2/1 LPC) twice, p1, k2, p2] twice, p1, k2, p2. ***46*** P2, 2/1 LPC, p2, [k2, 2/1 RPC, p2, 2/2 RC, p2, 2/1 LPC, k2, p2] twice, 2/1 RPC, p2. ***48*** P3, 2/1 LPC, SI-F, *p1, 2/1 RPC, 2/1 LPC, p1*, [SI-F] twice, work from * to * once, SI-F, 2/1 RPC, p3—44 sts. ***49*** K4, p2, k5, p2, k2, p2, k10, p2, k2, p2, k5, p2, k4. ***50*** P4, *2/1 LPC, p3, 2/1 RPC*, p2, 2/1 LPC, p8, 2/1 RPC, p2, work from * to * once, p4. ***51*** (WS) K5, 2/1 RPC, k2, p2, k4, 2/2 RPC, k4, 2/2 LPC, k4, p2, k2, 2/1 LPC, k5. ***52*** *P6, SI-G, p6*, SI-H, work from * to *—38 sts. ***53 and 55*** Knit. ***54*** Purl.

CHART B *OVER 15 STS*

Row 1 (WS) K3, p4, k2, p2, k2, p1, k1. ***2*** P1, k1, p2, 2/1 LPC, 2/1 RPC, 2/1 LPC, p2. ***3, 5, 7*** K the knit sts and p the purl sts. ***4*** P1, k1, p3, 2/2 LC, p2, k2, p2. ***6*** P1, k1, p2, 2/1 RPC, 2/1 LPC, 2/1 RPC, p2. ***8*** P1, k1, p2, k2, p2, 2/2 RC, p3. Rep rows 1–8 for Chart B.

Grafting open sts to cast-on sts

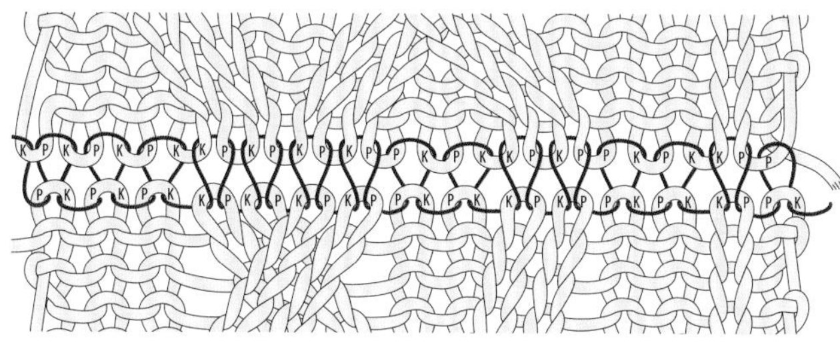

K = Draw yarn through st knitwise. P = Draw yarn through st purlwise.
(Remove st from needle when yarn has gone through st twice.)

VICKI SEVER

continued from p. 13

IN OTHER WORDS

CHART B *OVER 13 TO 23 TO 13 STS*

Row 1 (RS) P6, M1, Inc 2, M1, p6—17 sts. ***2*** (WS) K6, p2, Inc 2, p2, k6—19 sts. ***3*** P4, 2/2 RPC, k3, 2/2 LPC, p4. ***4*** K4, p2, k2, p3, k2, p2, k4. ***5*** P3, 2/1 RPC, p2, k3, p2, 2/1 LPC, p3. ***6*** K3, p2, k3, p3, k3, p2, k3. ***7*** M1, p2, 2/1 RPC, p1, M1, p2, k3, p2, M1, p1, 2/1 LPC, p2, M1—23 sts. ***8*** *P1, k2, p2, k2, p1*, k2, p3, k2, rep from * to * once. ***9*** 1/2 LPC, k2tog, 1/2 RPC, p2, k3, p2, 1/2 LPC, ssk, 1/2 RPC—21 sts. ***10*** K2, p3, k4, p3, k4, p3, k2. ***11*** P2, k3tog, p4, k3, p4, SK2P, p2—17 sts. ***12*** K7, p3, k7. ***13*** P4, MB, p2, k3, p2, MB, p4. ***14*** K4, p1, k2, p3, k2, p1, k4. ***15*** P4, 1/2 LPC, k3, 1/2 RPC, p4. ***16*** K6, p5, k6. ***17*** P6, 2/1/2 LPC, p6. ***18*** K6, p2, k1, p2, k6. ***19*** P4, 2/2 RPC, p1, 2/2 LPC, p4. ***20*** K4, p2, k5, p2, k4. ***21*** P4, 2/2 LPC, p1, 2/2 RPC, p4. ***22*** K6, p2, k1, p2, k6. ***23*** P6, Dec 4, p6—13 sts. ***24*** Knit.

CHART C *OVER 13 TO 21 TO 13 STS*

Row 1 (RS) P6, Inc 2, p6—15 sts. ***2*** (WS) K6, p1, Inc 2, p1, k6—17 sts. ***3*** P6, k2, p1, k2, p6. ***4*** K6, p2, k1, p2, k6. ***5*** P5, 2/1 RPC, k1, 2/1 LPC, p5. ***6*** K5, p2, k1, p1, k1, p2, k5. ***7*** P4, 2/1 RPC, k1, p1, k1, 2/1 LPC, p4. ***8*** K4, p2, [k1, p1] twice, k1, p2, k4. ***9*** P3, 2/1 RPC, [k1, p1] twice, k1, 2/1 LPC, p3. ***10*** K3, p2, [k1, p1] 3 times, k1, p2, k3. ***11*** P2, 2/1 RPC, [k1, p1] 3 times, k1, 2/1 LPC, p2. ***12*** K2, p2, [k1, p1] 4 times, k1, p2, k2. ***13*** 2/2 KPRC, [k1, p1] 4 times, k1, 2/2 PKLC. ***14*** P3, [k1, p1] 6 times, p2. ***15*** K2, [p1, k1] 7 times, k1. ***16*** P2, [k1, p1] 7 times, p1. ***17*** K2, [k1, p1] 3 times, Inc 2, [p1, k1] 3 times, k2—19 sts. ***18*** P3, [k1, p1] 3 times, Inc 2, [p1, k1] 3 times, p3—21 sts. ***19*** 2/1 LPC, [k1, p1] twice, 2/1 RPC, p1, 2/1 LPC, [p1, k1] twice, 2/1 RPC. ***20*** K1, p2, [p1, k1] twice, p2, k3, p2, [k1, p1] twice, p2, k1. ***21*** P1, 2/2 LPC, p1, 2/1 RPC, p3, 2/1 LPC, p1, 2/2 RPC, p1. ***22*** K3, p2, k1, p2, k5, p2, k1, p2, k3. ***23*** P3, Dec 4, p5, Dec 4, p3—13 sts. ***24*** Knit.

CHART D *OVER 13 TO 19 TO 13 STS*

Row 1 (RS) [K1, p1] 6 times, k1. ***2 and 3*** [P1, k1] 6 times, p1. ***4*** Rep row 1. ***5*** M1, Inc 2, [p1, k1] 5 times, p1, Inc 2, M1—19 sts. ***6*** P4, [k1, p1] 6 times, p3. ***7*** P1, k4, [p1, k1] 5 times, k3, p1. ***8 and all foll WS rows*** K the knit sts and p the purl sts. ***9*** K4, [p1, k1] 6 times, k3. ***11*** Rep row 7. ***13*** K1, 3/1 LPC, [k1, p1] 4 times, k1, 3/1 RPC, k1. ***15*** P1, k1, 3/1 LPC, [k1, p1] 3 times, k1, 3/1 RPC, k1, p1. ***17*** K1, p1, k1, 3/1 LPC, [k1, p1] twice, k1, 3/1 RPC, k1, p1, k1. ***19*** [P1, k1] twice, 3/1 LPC, k1, p1, k1, 3/1 RPC, [k1, p1] twice. ***21*** [K1, p1] twice, k1, 3/1 LPC, k1, 3/1 RPC, [k1, p1] twice, k1. ***23*** [P1, k1] 3 times, k3, p1, k3, [k1, p1] 3 times. ***25*** [K1, p1] 3 times, 3/1/3 RC, [p1, k1] 3 times. ***27*** [P1, k1] twice, p1, 3/1 RC, p1, 3/1 LC, [p1, k1] twice, p1. ***29*** [K1, p1] twice, 3/1 RC, p1, k1, p1, 3/1 LC, [p1, k1] twice. ***31*** P1, k1, p1, 3/1 RC, [p1, k1] twice, p1, 3/1 LC, p1, k1, p1. ***33*** K1, p1, 3/1 RC, [p1, k1] 3 times, p1, 3/1 LC, p1, k1. ***35*** P1, k4, [p1, k1] 4 times, p1, k4, p1. ***37*** K1, p1, k4, [p1, k1] 4 times, k3, p1, k1. ***39*** Rep row 15. ***41*** Rep row 17. ***43*** [P1, k1] twice, 3/2 PKLC, p1, 3/2 KPRC, [k1, p1] twice. ***45*** [K1, p1] 3 times, Dec 6, [p1, k1] 3 times—13 sts. ***47*** Rep row 2. ***48*** Rep row 1. ∩

SUZANNE ATKINSON

continued from p. 28

IN OTHER WORDS

CHART PAT *OVER 59 TO 63 TO 59 STS*

Row 1 (RS) P1, [k1 tbl, p1] 6 times, k6, [k1 tbl, p1] 3 times, k1 tbl, k4, p2, k2, p2, k6, p2, k2, p2, k4, p1, [k1 tbl, p1] 3 times. ***2*** K7, p4, k2, p2, k2, p6, k2, p2, k2, p4, k7, p6, k13. ***3*** P1, [k1 tbl, p1] 6 times, k6, [k1 tbl, p1] 3 times, k1 tbl, 2/2 LC, k2, p2, k10, p2, k2, 2/2 RC, p1, [k1 tbl, p1] 3 times. ***4*** K7, p6, k2, p10, k2, p6, k7, p6, k13. ***5-8*** Rep rows 1-4. ***9*** P1, [k1 tbl, p1] 6 times, k6, [k1 tbl, p1] 3 times, k1 tbl, k4, p2, k2, p2, k1, MSB, k4, p2, k2, p2, k4, p1, [k1 tbl, p1] 3 times. ***10-16*** Rep rows 2-8. ***17-18*** Rep rows 1-2. ***19*** P5, [k1 tbl, p1] 4 times, k6, [k1 tbl, p1] 3 times, k1 tbl, 2/2 LC, [k2, p2] 4 times, k2, 2/2 RC, p1, [k1 tbl, p1] 3 times. ***20*** K7, p6, [k2, p2] 4 times, p4, k7, p6, k13. ***21*** P7, [k1 tbl, p1] 3 times, k6, [k1 tbl, p1] 3 times, k1 tbl, k4, p2, [k2, p2] 4 times, k4, p1, [k1 tbl, p1] 3 times. ***22*** K7, p4, [k2, p2] 4 times, k2, p4, k7, p6, k13. ***23*** P9, [k1 tbl, p1] twice, M1K, k6, M1K, [k1 tbl, p1] 3 times, k1 tbl, 2/2 LC, [k2, p2] 4 times, k2, 2/2 RC, p1, [k1 tbl, p1] 3 times—61 sts. ***24*** K7, p6, [k2, p2] 4 times, p4, k7, p8, k13. ***25*** P13, k1, M1K, k6, M1K, k1, [k1 tbl, p1] 3 times, k1 tbl, M1P, k4, p2tog, [k2, p2] 3 times, k2, p2tog, k4, M1P, p1, [k1 tbl, p1] 3 times—63 sts. ***26*** K8, p4, k1, p2, [k2, p2] 3 times, k1, p4, k8, p10, k13. ***27*** P11, 2/2 RPC, k6, 2/2 LPC, p6, M1P, 2/2 LC, p2tog, p1, [k2, p2] twice, k2, p1, p2tog, 2/2 RC, M1P, p2, [k1 tbl, p1] 3 times. ***28*** K9, p4, [k2, p2] 3 times, k2, p4, k7, p2, k2, p6, k2, p2, k11. ***29*** P9, 2/2 RPC, p2, k6, p2, 2/2 LPC, p5, M1P, k4, p2tog, p2, [k2, p2] twice, p2tog, k4, M1P, p9. ***30*** K10, p4, k3, [p2, k2] twice, k1, p4, k6, p2, k4, p6, k4, p2, k9. ***31*** P7, 2/2 RPC, p4, k6, p4, 2/2 LPC, p4, M1P, 2/2 LC, p2tog, k1, p2, k2, p2, k1, p2tog, 2/2 RC, M1P, p10. ***32*** K11, p4, k1, p1, k2, p2, k2, p1, k1, p4, k5, p2, k6, p6, k6, p2, k7. ***33*** P7, k2, p4, 2/2 RPC, k2, 2/2 LPC, p4, k2, p5, M1P, k4, p2tog, k2, p2, k2, p2tog, k4, M1P, p11. ***34*** K12, p4, k1, p2, k2, p2, k1, p4, k6, p2, k4, [p2, k2] twice, p2, k4, p2, k7. ***35*** P6, 1/1 RPC, k1 tbl, p2, 2/2 RPC, p2, k2, p2, 2/2 LPC, p2, k1 tbl, 1/1 LPC, p5, M1P, 2/2 LC, p2tog, p1, k2, p1, p2tog, 2/2 RC, M1P, p12. ***36*** K13, p4, k2, p2, k2, p4, k6, p1, k1, p1, k2, [p2, k4] twice, p2, k2, p1, k1, p1, k6. ***37*** P5, 1/1 RPC, p1, MB, p2, k2, [p4, k2] twice, p2, MB, p1, 1/1 LPC, p5, M1P, k4, p2tog, p2, p2tog, k4, M1P, p13. ***38*** K14, p4, k4, p4, k6, p1, k5, [p2, k4] twice, p2, k5, p1, k5. ***39*** [P4, 1/1 RPC] twice, k1 tbl, p4, k2, p4, k1 tbl, [1/1 LPC, p4] twice, p1, M1P, 2/2 LPC, [p2tog] twice, 2/2 RPC, M1P, p14. ***40*** K17, p2, k2, p2, k8, p1, k5, p1, k1, p1, k4, p2, k4, p1, k1, p1, k5, p1, k4. ***41*** P2, p2tog, MB, p4, 1/1 RPC, p1, MB, p3, 1/1 RPC, 1/1 LPC, p3, MB, p1, 1/1 LPC, p4, MB, p2tog, p6, M1P, k1, ssk, k2tog, k1, M1P, p17—61 sts. ***42*** K18, p4, k13, p1, k6, p1, k2, p1, k6, p1, k8. ***43*** P7, 1/1 RPC, p5, 1/1 RPC, p2, 1/1 LPC, p5, 1/1 LPC, p12, 2/2 LC, p18. ***44*** K6, p2, k10, p4, k12, p1, k6, p1, k4, p1, k6, p1, k7. ***45*** P5, p2tog, MB, p5, 1/1 RPC, p4, 1/1 LPC, p5, MB, p2tog, p10, k4, p10, sl 2 with yarn in back (wyib), p6—59 sts. ***46*** K6, sl 2 with yarn in front (wyif), k10, p4, k17, p1, k6, p1, k12. ***47*** P12, MB, p6, MB, p17, 2/2 LC, p8, 1/2 RPC, 1/2 LPC, p4. ***48 and 50*** K18, p4, k37. ***49*** P37, k4, p18. ***51*** P37, 2/2 PKLC, p18. ***52*** K19, p2, k38. ***53*** P38, k2, p19. ***54*** K9, p2, k8, p2, k38. ***55*** P16, M1K, Inc 2, M1K, p21, k2, p8, sl 2 wyib, p9—63 sts. ***56*** K9, sl 2 wyif, k8, p2, k21, p2, k1, p2, k16. ***57*** P14, 2/2 RPC, p1, 2/2 LPC, p19, k2, p6, 1/2 RPC, 1/2 LPC, p7. ***58*** K19, p2, k19, p2, k5, p2, k14. ***59*** P13, 2/1 RPC, p5, 2/1 LPC, p15, k8, p16. ***60*** K16, p8, k15, p2, k7, p2, k13. ***61*** P13, k2, p7, k2, p15, k8, p16. ***62*** K19, p2, k18, p2, k7, p2, k13. ***63*** P13, 2/1 LPC, p5, 2/1 RPC, p18, k2, p19. ***64*** K6, p2, k11, p2, k19, p2, k5, p2, k14. ***65*** P14, 2/2 LPC, p1, 2/2 RPC, p19, k2, p11, sl 2 wyib, p6. ***66*** K6, sl 2 wyif, k34, Dec 4, k16—59 sts. ***67*** P49, 1/2 RPC, 1/2 LPC, p4.

KATHLEEN T. CARTY

continued from p. 11

IN OTHER WORDS

CHART C *WORKED OVER 19 STS TO 1 ST*

Row 1 (RS) K5, p3, k4, p3, k2, p2. ***2*** (WS) K2, p2, k3, p4, k3, p2, k3. ***3*** K3, 1/1 RC, p3, 2/2 LC, p3, 1/1 LC, p2. ***4 and all foll WS rows (except 40, 42 and 44)*** K the knit sts and p the purl sts to last 3 sts, k3. ***5*** K5, p2, 2/1 RPC, 2/1 LPC, p2, k2, p2. ***7*** K3, 1/1 RC, p1, 2/1 RPC, p2, 2/1 LPC, p1, 1/1 LC, p2. ***9*** K5, p1, k2, p4, k2, p1, k2, p2. ***11*** K3, 1/1 RC, p1, 2/1 LPC, p2, 2/1 RPC, p1, 1/1 LC, p2. ***13*** K5, p2, 2/1 LPC, 2/1 RPC, p2, k2, p2. ***15*** Rep row 3. ***17*** Rep row 1. ***19*** K3, 1/1 RC, p3, 2/2 LC, p3, 1/1 LC, W&T. ***21*** K5, p2, 2/1 RPC, 2/1 LPC, p2, W&T. ***23*** K3, 1/1 RC, p1, 2/1 RPC, p2, 2/1 LPC, W&T. ***25*** K5, p1, k2, p4, k1, W&T. ***27*** K3, 1/1 RC, p1, k2, p3, W&T. ***29*** K5, p1, k2, p2, W&T. ***31*** K3, 1/1 RC, p1, k2, p1, W&T. ***33*** K5, p1, k1, W&T. ***35*** K3, 1/1 RC, p1, W&T. ***37*** K5, W&T. ***39*** K3, W&T. ***40*** K3. ***41*** K2, W&T. ***42*** K2. ***43*** K1, W&T. ***44*** K1.

CHART D *WORKED OVER 2 STS TO 19 STS*

Row 1 (RS) K1, W&T. ***2*** K1. ***3*** K1, HKW, W&T. ***4*** K2. ***5*** K2, HKW, W&T. ***6*** K3. ***7*** K3, 1/1 HWRC, W&T. ***8 and all foll WS rows*** K the knit sts and p the purl sts to last 3 sts, k3. ***9*** K5, HPW, W&T. ***11*** K3, 1/1 RC, p1, HKW, W&T. ***13*** K5, p1, k1, HKW, p1, W&T. ***15*** K3, 1/1 RC, p1, k2, p1, HPW, W&T. ***17*** K5, p1, k2, p2, HPW, W&T. ***19*** K3, 1/1 RC, p1, k2, p3, HPW, k1, W&T. ***21*** K5, p1, k2, p4, k1, HKW, W&T. ***23*** K3, 1/1 RC, p1, k2, p4, k2, HPW, W&T. ***25*** K5, p1, k2, p4, k2, p1, HKW, k1, W&T. ***27*** K3, 1/1 RC, p1, 2/1 LPC, p2, 2/1 RPC, p1, 1/1 LC, HPW, p1. ***29*** K5, p2, 2/1 LPC, 2/1 RPC, p2, k2, p2. ***31*** K3, 1/1 RC, p3, 2/2 RC, p3, 1/1 LC, p2. ***33*** K5, p3, k4, p3, k2, p2. ***35*** Rep row 31. ***37*** K5, p2, 2/1 RPC, 2/1 LPC, p2, k2, p2. ***39*** K3, 1/1 RC, p1, 2/1 RPC, p2, 2/1 LPC, p1, 1/1 LC, p2. ***41*** K5, p1, k2, p4, k2, p1, k2, p2. ***43*** K3, 1/1 RC, p1, 2/1 LPC, p2, 2/1 RPC, p1, 1/1 LC, p2. ***45*** Rep row 29. ***47*** Rep row 31. ***48*** Rep row 8. ∩

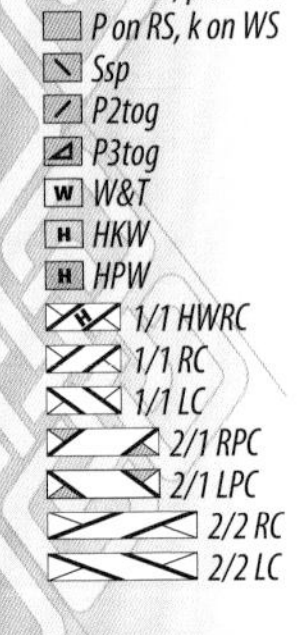

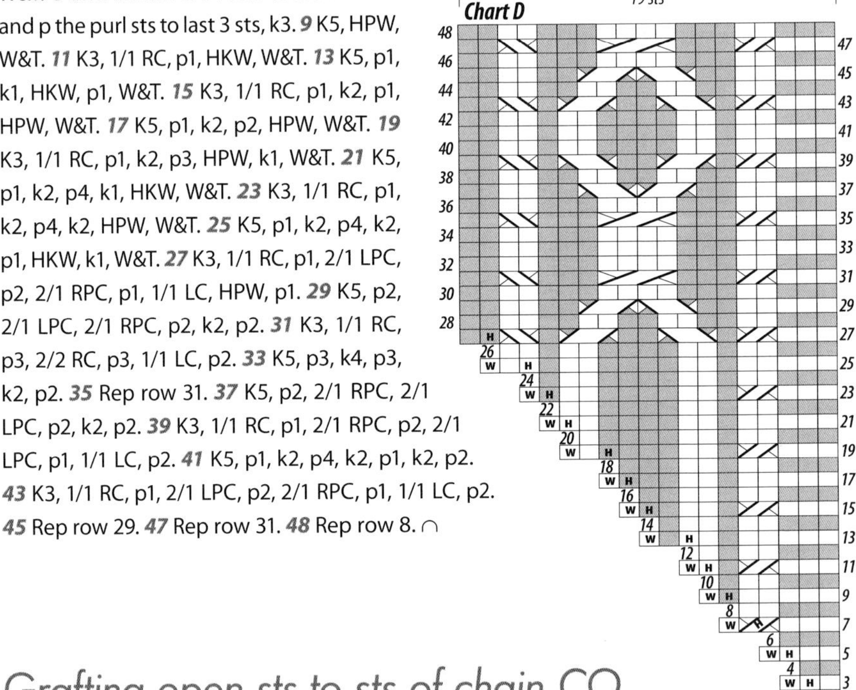

Grafting open sts to sts of chain CO

Run cast-on tail through loop at edge to create an extra stitch.

K = *Draw yarn through st knitwise.* P = *Draw yarn through st purlwise.*
(Remove st from needle when yarn has gone through st twice.)

Finishing

Because the squares have different numbers of stitches and rows, seaming them together is an exercise in patience and skill. Take the count of the ridges or stitches at a join, and join with an overcast stitch, easing the difference evenly along the join. Once you've joined three or four squares, the rest is a breeze. Keep the stitching neat, but not too tight so the seam remains as pliable as the fabric.

We've added a cable stitch border to the afghan and pillows. The stitch is easy and effective. Six cable twists edge each block. A simple short row treatment is used to turn the corners.

You may need to purchase an additional ball of yarn to complete the pillows.

AFGHAN BORDER

Cast on 16 sts. *Work rows 1–14 of Afghan Border Chart 30 times, then work rows 1–28 of Afghan Corner Chart, work rows 1–14 of Afghan Border Chart 24 times, rows 1–28 of Afghan Corner Chart; rep from* once more. Place sts on hold. Sew on border. Graft open sts to cast-on row.

PILLOW BORDER

Cast on 20 sts. Work rows 1–14 of Pillow Border Chart 24 times. Graft open sts to cast-on row, being careful not to twist border. Place 4 markers evenly spaced along edge and sew border to square, matching corners of square to markers. Rep on other edge of border with a 2nd square, placing pillow form prior to seaming final side. ∩

GRAFTING OPEN STS TO CAST-ON EDGE

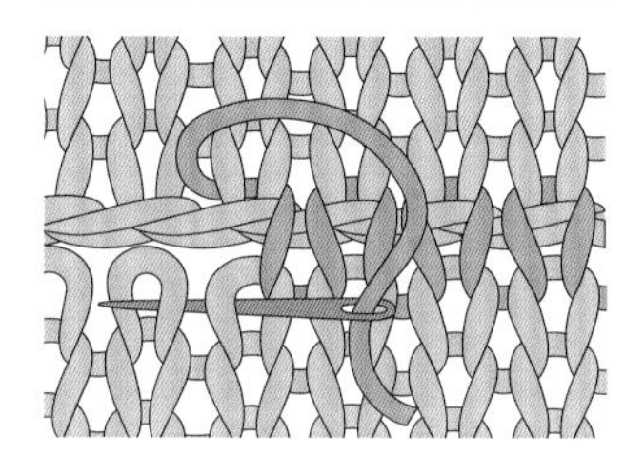

Needles Size 4.5mm (US 7)

Extras Two 14" pillow forms
Cable needle (cn)

IN OTHER WORDS

6/6 RC Sl 6 to cn, hold to back, k6; k6 from cn.
WRAP ST & TURN (W&T) With yarn in back, sl 1 to RH needle, bring yarn to front between needles, sl st back to LH needle, turn work.
HIDE WRAPS (HW) K 3 wraps tog with st on LH needle.

AFGHAN BORDER CHART
OVER 16 STS
Row 1 and all RS rows (except 13) (RS) K16. ***2 and all WS rows*** K4, p12. ***13*** 6/6 RC, k4. ***14*** Rep row 2. Rep rows 1–14 for Afghan Border Chart.

AFGHAN CORNER CHART
OVER 16 STS
Rows 1 and 3 (RS) K16. ***2, 4*** K4, p12. ***5, 7, 9*** K12, W&T. ***6, 8, 10*** P12. ***11*** K12, HW, k3. ***12, 14*** K4, p12. ***13*** 6/6 RC, k4. ***15-22*** Rep rows 5-12. ***23, 25*** K16. ***24, 26, 28*** K4, p12. ***27*** 6/6 RC, k4.

PILLOW BORDER CHART
OVER 20 STS
Row 1 and all RS rows (except 13) (RS) K20. ***2 and all WS rows*** K4, p12, k4. ***13*** K4, 6/6 RC, k4. ***14*** Rep row 2. Rep rows 1-14 for Pillow Border Chart.

Afghan Border Chart

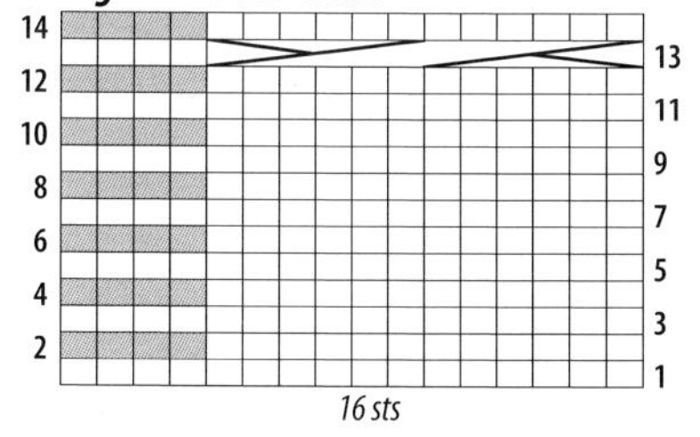

Afghan Corner Chart

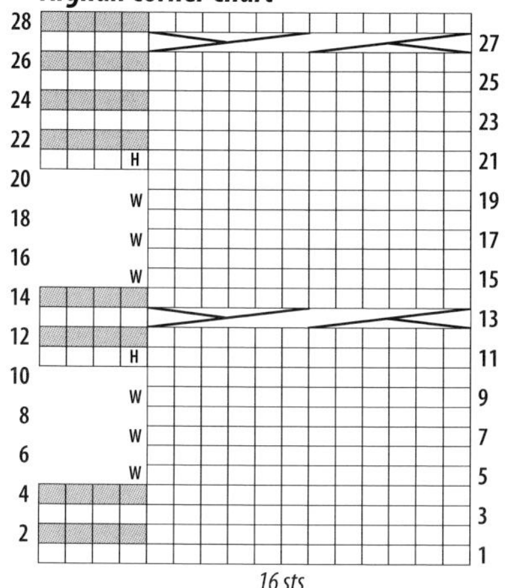

□ *K on RS, p on WS* ▩ *K on WS*
6/6 RC
W *Wrap st & turn (W&T)*
H *Hide wraps (HW)*

Pillow Border Chart

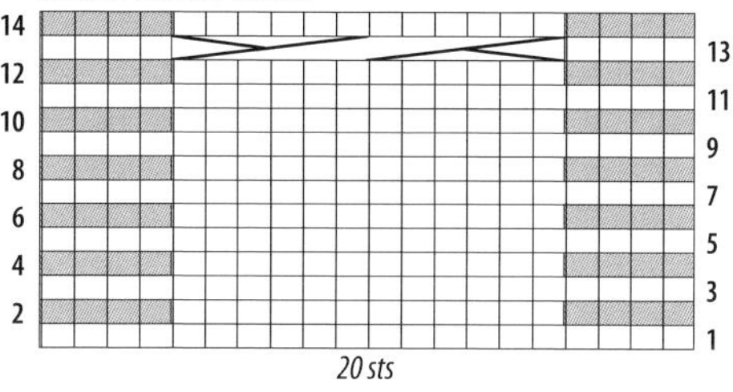

Knitter's School

abbreviations

approx approximate(ly)
b in back of stitch
beg begin(ning)(s)
CC contrasting color
cn cable needle
cm centimeter(s)
cont continu(e)(ed)(es)(ing)
dec decreas(e)(ed)(es)(ing)
dpn double-pointed needle(s)
foll follow(s)(ing)
g gram(s)
" inch(es)
inc increas(e)(ed)(es)(ing)
k knit(ting)(s)(ted)
LH left-hand
LC left cross (cable)
LPC left purl cross (cable)
M1 make one
m meter(s)
MC main color
oz ounce(s)
p purl(ed)(ing)(s)
pat(s) pattern(s)
pm place marker
psso pass slipped stitch(es) over
rem remain(s)(ing)
rep repeat(s)
rev reverse(d)
RC right cross (cable)
RH right-hand
RPC purl purl cross (cable)
RS right side(s)
rnd round(s)
sc single crochet
sl slip(ped)(ping)
skp slip, knit, psso
ssk slip, slip, knit 2tog
st(s) stitch(es)
St st stockinette stitch
TLPC twist left purl cable
TRPC twist right purl cable
tbl through back of loop(s)
tog together
WS wrong side(s)
wyib with yarn in back
wyif with yarn in front
yd yard(s)
yo (2) yarn over (twice)

metrics

To convert the inches measurements used in our instructions to centimeters, simply multiply the inches by 2.5.
For example: 4" x 2.5 = 10cm

Charts and symbols

Our charts show the right side (RS) of the fabric. In general, each "square" is a stitch; a row of squares represents a row (or round) of stitches. Heavy lines on the charts are used to define pattern repeats. RS: When facing the RS of the fabric, read the chart from right to left as you work and work the stitches as the symbols indicate. If you are working circularly, work every round thus. WS: If you are working back and forth in rows, every other row will be a wrong side (WS) row. Read WS rows from left to right as you work.

INVISIBLE CAST-ON

Uses As a *temporary cast-on*, when access to the bottom loops is needed: to knit, graft, attach a border, or for an elastic hem.

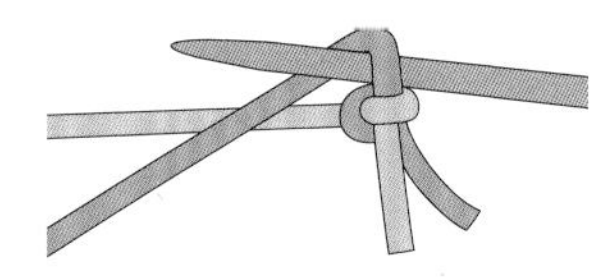

1 Knot working yarn to contrasting waste yarn. With needle in right hand, hold knot in right hand. Tension both strands in left hand; separate the strands with fingers of the left hand. Yarn over with working yarn in front of waste strand.

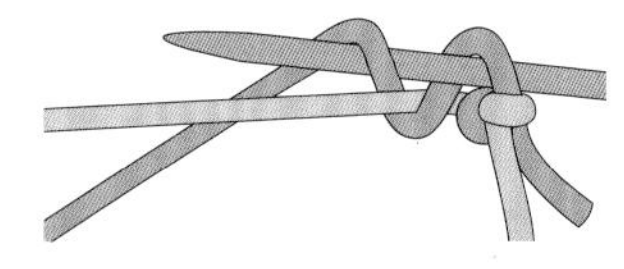

2 Holding waste strand taut, pivot yarns, and yarn over with working yarn in back of waste strand.
3 Each yarn over forms a stitch. Alternate yarn over in front and in back of waste strand for required number of stitches. For an even number, twist working yarn around waste strand before knitting the first row.
Later, untie knot, remove waste strand, and arrange bottom loops on needle.

GRAFTING

Uses An invisible method of joining knitting horizontally, row to row. Useful at shoulders, underarms, and tips of mittens, socks, and hats.

Stockinette graft

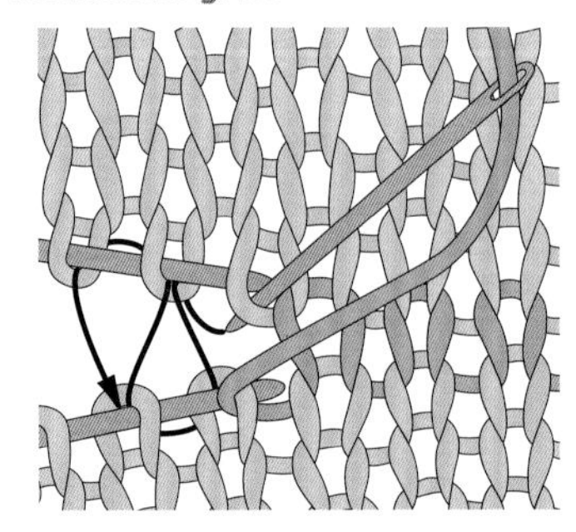

1 Arrange stitches on two needles.
2 Thread a blunt needle with matching yarn (approximately 1" per stitch).
3 Working from right to left, with right sides facing you, begin with Steps 3a and 3b:
3a Front needle: yarn through 1st stitch as if to purl, leave stitch on needle.
3b Back needle: yarn through 1st stitch as if to knit, leave on.
4 Work 4a and 4b across:
4a Front needle: through 1st stitch as if to knit, slip off needle; through next st as if to purl, leave on needle.
4b Back needle: through 1st stitch as if to purl, slip off needle; through next st as if to knit, leave on needle.
5 Adjust tension to match rest of knitting.

MAKE 1 KNIT (M1K)

Uses A single increase.

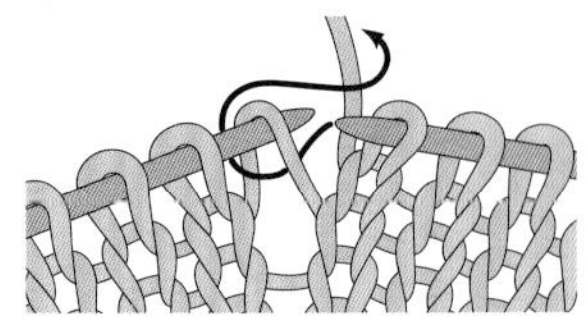

1 For a *left-slanting increase* (M1L), with right needle from back of work, pick up strand between last st knitted and next st. Place on left needle and knit, twisting the strand by working into the loop at the back of the needle.

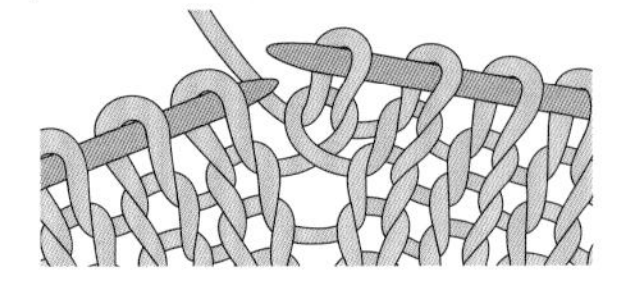

2 This is the completed increase.

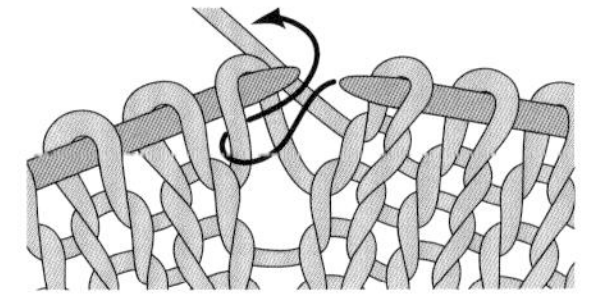

3 Or, for a right-slanting increase (M1R), with left needle from back of work, pick up strand between last stitch knitted and next stitch. Knit, twisting the strand by working into the loop at the front of the needle.

MAKE 1 (M1) PURL

Left-slanting: Work as for Make 1 Knit, Step 1, except purl, twisting the strand by working into the back loop.
Right-slanting: Work as for Make 1 Knit, Step 3, except purl.

SSK

Uses A left-slanting single decrease.

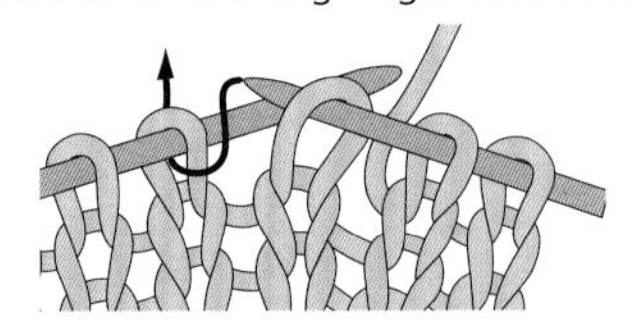

1 Slip 2 sts separately to right needle as if to knit.

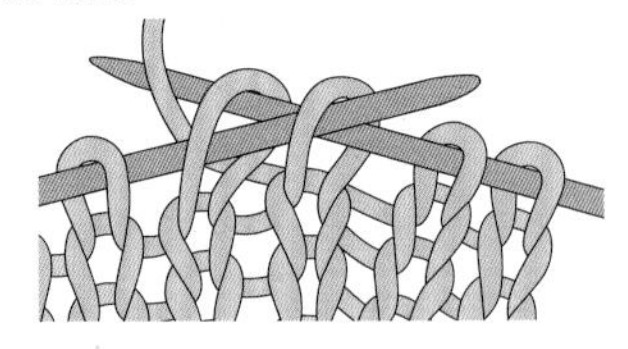

2 Knit these 2 sts together by slipping left needle into them from left to right.

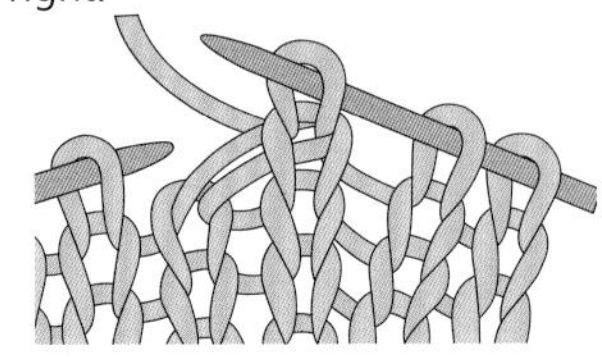

SKP, SL 1-K1-PSSO

Uses A left-slanting single decrease.
1 Slip one stitch knitwise.
2 Knit next stitch.
3 Pass the slipped stitch over knit stitch.